When the Buddha Needs Therapy

Keith Martin-Smith

INTEGRAL
LIFE
PRESS

Copyright © 2022 by Keith Martin-Smith

All rights reserved. Published in the United States of America. No part of this book may be reproduced or transmitted in any form or by any means, graphic, electronic or mechanical, including photocopying, recording, taping or by any information storage or retrieval system, without permission in writing from the publisher.

This edition published by Integral Life Press,
an imprint of Highpoint Executive Publishing.
For information, write to info@highpointpubs.com.

First Edition

ISBN: 978-1-7372886-9-5

Library of Congress Cataloging-in-Publication Data

Martin-Smith, Keith
When the Buddha Needs Therapy

Summary: "Your deepest contraction and your biggest fears are the places where liberation lies, not in heaven or nirvana or some far-away perfect and enlightened place, but here, now. You can't be freed from this world, but you can be freed within it and, paradoxically, then be freed from it. This book will explain how." – Provided by publisher.

Excerpts from *The Heart of Zen: Enlightenment, Emotional Maturity, and What It Really Takes for Spiritual Liberation* by Jun Po Denis Kelly Roshi and Keith Martin-Smith, published by North Atlantic Books, copyright © 2014 by Jun Po Denis Kelly Roshi and Keith Martin-Smith. Reprinted by permission of North Atlantic Books.

ISBN: 978-1-7372886-9-5 (paperback)
Self-Help, Spiritualism

Library of Congress Control Number: 2022907198

Cover art of the Buddha getting therapy by Mark T. Smith. All rights reserved.

Interior design by Sarah M. Clarehart

Manufactured in the United States of America

Publisher's Note

One of the missions of Integral Life Press is to publish books on important aspects of Integral Philosophy that deserve rich, book-length explorations. This book is no exception. We live at a time when our personal and social identities have never been as central, or controversial, to the human lifeworld. We also live at a time when existential dread, hopeful resolve, and social tumult all mix to expose the depth, and limitations, of our collective spiritual maturity in the twenty-first century. Keith Martin-Smith carries us into the heart of advanced modern spiritual understanding, exposing the relationship between the timebound, perspective-generating ego, and the timeless, aperspectival Self of classic mysticism.

In Integral Philosophy, we call these two faces of the spiritual journey the "growing up" of *vertical enlightenment*, and the "waking up" of *horizontal enlightenment* (vertical because the process is developmental, thus over the temporal life course, and horizontal because it's timeless, always right now). This tension – between the natural, egoic, embodied process that is our identity, and the awake spiritual being that is beyond our identity – remains one of the most confusing areas of spiritual development for many people today.

Enter Martin-Smith's call for us to awaken *through* our uniqueness by integrating the two most powerful forces of liberation available to us:

the psychotherapeutic work of healing our wounds, a process of "cleaning up" past traumas and egoic conditioning that can, when combined with more classical awakening work, generate an integral spiritual wholeness that is available in no other way. Every being a Buddha, and every Buddha needs therapy.

Given the stakes of the challenges and division we face this century, this is a spiritual wholeness we urgently need to foster, starting with ourselves. And this book will help you do so.

Robb Smith
August, 2022

TABLE OF CONTENTS

Foreword	vii
About This Book	1
Chapter 1: The Problem with a Spiritual Identity	5
Chapter 2: What Is Spiritual, Anyway?	27
Chapter 3: The Dignity and the Disaster of Our Egos	49
Chapter 4: When the Buddha Needs Therapy	67
Chapter 5: No One Has Ever Made You Angry (Really)	87
Chapter 6: Why There Are No Victims in Zen	103
Chapter 7: Can You Choose Enlightenment?	119
Chapter 8: Enlightening	143
Postscript: My Dark Night of the Self	151
Acknowledgments	157
About the Author	159
Index	161

Foreword

One of my wiser professors in graduate school said that there were advantages to filtering knowledge through many different minds. He said there were also advantages to integrating knowledge within a single mind. This has proved to be true and helpful over the years for me, especially when it comes to knowledge. However, this book is not about knowledge, it is about what the author calls "Enlightening," which relates to insight, discernment, wisdom, and awakening. It is also a deep look into the teachings of a great Zen Master—Junpo Denis Kelly Roshi (1942-2021)—that were received, integrated, and further evolved by a single mind, the mind of the author.

Keith Martin-Smith was not only one of Junpo Kando Roshi's senior students, but he is also an award-winning author of two books written about and with Junpo. *A Heart Blown Open* (2012) was Junpo's spiritual biography, while *The Heart of Zen* (2014) articulated Junpo's deepest wisdom through his teaching of Mondo Zen. In both books, Keith brought Junpo's insight and wisdom into the world in a powerful way. In this book, Keith begins the articulation of his own insights and more integral understanding of Junpo's teaching, revealing how those teachings have taken root, grown, and are beginning to flower in Keith's own body, mind, and life.

One of the provocative teachings of Junpo was, "The only trouble with Zen, and with psychotherapy, is they don't work." Junpo was indeed a troublemaker. He loved to throw emotionally charged hand grenades like this one into a crowd, and then step back and bare witness, making note of who got triggered, and why. This was one of Junpo's most skillful means. It was a tool and he used it like a fishing pole as he hooked, with unparalleled mastery, many of his students and then released them into the community where he could teach them—about insight, about emotional maturity, and about proper stewardship of all their relationships, with sentient and non-sentient beings. He was incredibly skilled at this method.

I was hooked several years before Keith, and I was able to witness the process of Keith first being hooked, receiving these powerful teachings, and then helping Junpo disseminate them through two books. And now one year after Junpo's death, I am delighted to write this foreword because Keith is breathing new life into Junpo's original teachings for the next generation. But be careful, for as Keith warns: "Your biggest triggers and your deepest fears are the places where enlightening begins."

Junpo's core teaching of Mondo Zen is clearly articulated in *The Heart of Zen*. It consists of two separate processes. First the Ego Deconstruction Process, followed by the Emotional Koan Process. Keith lives and works in Boulder, Colorado where most people you encounter on the street consider themselves to be "spiritual," but not "religious." This is a most interesting and tenacious form of new age (postmodern) spiritual identity that must begin to be deconstructed before the process of awakening, or Enlightening, can even begin. Keith wisely avoids the messy quagmire of Junpo's emotional koans, which too many of Junpo's postmodern students reduced into a superficial addiction to feeling good rather than a means of true liberation from ego confusion and suffering.

In this book Keith is presenting a more evolved form of Junpo's Mondo Zen Process, in a voice uniquely his own, to reach an audience that most desperately needs it. The process of deconstructing the postmodern collective spiritual identity is a crucial beginning point to heal the collective illnesses of those who are stuck in victim mentality as well as those whose spiritual identity is pretending to be some heroic rescuer of all victims. Keith cuts through this dualistic conflict of false spiritual identity and dysfunctional victim mentality with Manjushri's sword. He swings the sword, distilling Junpo's emotional koan into one statement of diamond clarity: "There are no victims in Zen." No victims, no suffering.

As you are reading, remember that this book is specifically written for those who want to step onto a path of "enlightening." Be warned, the first step on this path is the deconstruction of your precious "spiritual identity." So, proceed with caution and persistence, for this book may at first seem problematic for certain readers. For those who want to feed or inflate their "spiritual identity," and for those who need to pretend they always feel good, their defenses will rise up to meet this challenge to their tightly held views. The hidden issue with pretending to always feel good is it requires us to suppress all bad feelings. Ignoring half of our feelings automatically creates and reinforces a false spiritual identity. This book can also present moral dilemmas for those who see themselves as "spiritual entrepreneurs," who try to enhance their spiritual identity by increasing their wealth and status by selling the Dharma—reflecting their lack of penetrating insight and egolessness in the face of a truly earth-shattering awakening. (Selling the Dharma reflects a lack of insight into the negative karma and suffering it can cause because the selling negates the very process needed to fully awaken.) So, if you get triggered by anything in this book, take a breath, get curious about the gold buried under your discomfort, and keep reading!

Keith is standing on groundless ground articulating, in his own voice, the essence of his teacher's teaching. He is talking to a specific collective group—those who are imprisoned by their addiction to their own spiritual identities and infected with feelings of helplessness. These two issues are plaguing whole generations today, infecting them with the toxic shame of being helplessly stuck in victim mentality without any hope of healing or attaining freedom. Keith has provided a brilliant, implicitly integral perspective that invites each reader to step into a bigger and deeper view of the world and themselves. And of course, the invitation can only be accepted by those who have the ears to hear and the tongue to taste the deepest truth of who we are. For those who have successfully accepted or been called by the invitation to experience this "Buddha Nature" for themselves, remember Keith's profound discernment that transcends Junpo's idea of an emotional koan: This embodiment of Buddha Nature, once tasted, will still need significant, ego-based psychotherapy to completely awaken for the benefit of all beings. Because the Buddha (that's you and me) does indeed need therapy.

Doshin Michael Nelson Roshi,
Abbot and Founder, Integral Zen

To Junpo, teacher and friend

About This Book

My teacher, Junpo Denis Kelly Roshi, was a Rinzai Zen master. As such, he often said things intended to irritate listeners in a way that would cause them to reflect more deeply on their beliefs. It is our beliefs, more than anything, that obscure us from the deeper clarity sought through a spiritual practice.

One of his favorite sayings was, "The only trouble with Zen, and with psychotherapy, is they don't work." That is a very interesting thing for a Zen master and lineage holder to say, especially one who was the head abbot of his own school of Zen, and who spent many years in ongoing forms of psychotherapy, even well into his later 60s. He did this to better understand his own childhood trauma and how it continued to impact his day-to-day life.

As was so often the case with his provocative sayings, there was an implied wink in the ridiculousness of the statement itself. Nevertheless, it had the dual benefit of pissing off all the spiritual practitioners in the room along with all of the therapists—no small feat. In a place like Boulder, Colorado, where I live, that often meant just about everyone in the room! And yet his message had a serious point behind it: There is no awakening without bringing your ego—and all of its shadows, blind spots, conditioning, and neurotic tics—along for the ride. And there is no therapy in the world that can awaken you from your suffering. These two things, therapy and spiritual practice, don't really work—unless you use them together.

Therapy, in part, tries to strengthen our egoic identity to one that is healthy and strong, can integrate its traumas, and is able to reflect on the ways it's prone to deceiving itself. *Spirituality*, in part, tries to soften our egoic identity to one that is transparent and open to seeing beyond its beliefs and opinions about reality, a reality that is utterly unconcerned with our view—our opinion—of it.

As such, this book will begin with the challenge of our egoic identities, and how those identities—especially if they're spiritual—can be the thing most in the way of awakening. We'll then move into how childhood conditioning and trauma can greatly complicate our spiritual practice, and how that spiritual practice is unable to help us see and face our psychological shadows.

If this book were to be reduced to a single sentence, it would be this: *We awaken through our egos, not from them.*

We live in interesting times. Identity has burst upon our collective consciousness. Identity politics. Racial and gender identities. Polarized electorates waging war against identities not like their own. Pro-mask and anti-mask identities. Spiritual identities, woke identities, conservative identities, progressive identities, national identities, scientific identities, religious identities, postmodern identities. Identities that create ideologies and then attach to those ideologies creating the endless war we find in our world, and inside of ourselves.

Yet there is a fundamental truth of our universe that stopped me in my tracks the moment I realized it. It seems that some billions of years ago there was nothing. Or rather, there was nothing except, somehow, the potential for all of this, but there was no time, no space, no laws of the universe, nothing except…some kind of suchness, some kind of potentiality. "Before the Big Bang" doesn't even make sense because there was no time before then, so

ABOUT THIS BOOK

how could there be anything *before*? We don't know and we can't know, at least not with our thinking brains. Our rational minds and our intellects are like computers fed bad data. We look at the birth of the universe, or inside of black holes, and it generates an error code in our brains. How do we conceive of things that don't exist in time, in space, in the reality that seems so…real to us?

The most cutting-edge science tells us that a paradox lives at the core of this universe and that paradox seems to be beyond mathematics, reason, or even imagination. Science, in short, is unable to even approach, much less explain, the foundational truth of the universe: First there was Nothing and then, somehow, there was Something.

There is another way to know this paradox, however, one that is outside of our thinking minds and the computational parts of our brains.

There is a way to know the grand, ultimate truth of the universe, and to know it deeply inside of ourselves, as ourselves.

There is a way to live inside of the paradox of what is and to live as this paradox, and in so doing free ourselves from the endless wars inside and out.

For many thousands of years, a small number of very wise humans have cracked this riddle of our existence, but they've done so not with their thinking minds at all, but their direct apprehension of *what is, now*.

> *Empty your mind of all thoughts. Let your heart be at peace. Watch the turmoil of beings, but contemplate their return.*
>
> *Each separate being in the universe returns to this common source. Returning to the source is serenity.*
>
> *If you don't realize this source, you stumble in confusion and sorrow. When you realize where you come from, you naturally become tolerant, disinterested, amused, kindhearted as a grandmother, dignified as a king.*
>
> *Immersed in the wonder of the Tao, you can deal with whatever life brings you, and when death comes, you are ready.*[1] *—Master Lao Tzu, 600 B.C.E.*

---

1 *Tao Te Ching*, trans. Stephen Mitchell (New York: Harper Perennial Modern Classics, 1988).

This book is not a work of philosophy. It is certainly not a standard self-help book, or a book on spirituality *per se*. Or therapy. It resides in the canon of Zen, which is to say it's merely offering you a view.

It is possible to be liberated from the suffering of this world, but the path to doing it is a paradoxical one, like the universe itself. In the end, it comes down to choice. If you seek liberation and freedom from the endless strife and suffering of your mind and of our world, continue.

But be warned: There is no waking up outside of this world. Liberation comes only through the door of you and into the places you are most trying to avoid, right now. Your deepest contraction and your biggest fears are the places where liberation lies—not in heaven or nirvana or some faraway perfect and enlightened place, but here, now. You can't be freed from this world, but you can be freed within it and, paradoxically, then be freed from it.

This book will explain how.

Keith Martin-Smith

CHAPTER 1

The Problem with a Spiritual Identity

If you consider yourself *spiritual*, you might be moving away from your goal. In fact, that's almost certainly the case.

We all know people who are a little *too* identified with their spiritualty. You know the types. The ones who describe themselves as *empaths* and *lightworkers* but seem like they would benefit more from a few psychotherapy sessions than another cacao ceremony. Or the spiritual seekers who always seem to be chasing another spiritual experience, be it through ayahuasca, retreats, workshops, or an endless consumption of books—as their ability to be fully in *this* world seems to grow more tenuous. And we have the Zen students who think they've transcended reactivity but who feel *cold* and *detached* instead of *awake* and *alive*. There are more types than this, of course, from the sanctimonious and hypocritical Christian, to the New Age devotee who has either abandoned reason or never knew it in the first place. With all these kinds of people it seems possible that for many, their identity as a "spiritual" person might actually be in the way of their spiritual growth. It's a delicious irony worthy of a Russian novelist.

Unfortunately, it's not that different with us.

If you have a spiritual practice, be it yoga, meditation, prayer, nature mysticism, contemplation, or some kind of conscious practice that you define as "spiritual," then you may be heaping a whole bunch of expectations on yourself, your community, and your experiences. These expectations could be undermining the very thing you're seeking inside of your practice, which is some kind of deeper expression of and connection to "source" (God, Jesus, oneness, nature, enlightenment, heart, divine feminine or masculine, or something else "beyond" ego).

Considering yourself spiritual could be as innocuous as believing there *might* be "something rather than nothing" behind the undeniable beauty and complexity of the universe in which we find ourselves, we curiously self-aware little hominids. That would hardly rise to a problematic view of spirituality or one that's likely to get in your way.

Most of us get into spirituality at least in part because we reject religion, with its dogma and its outdated rules, but also reject atheism and scientific reductionism, which insists (sometime with a religious fervor) that life is nothing more than random chance and luck. Many of us self-identified spiritual people would, I think, say that being spiritual helps us find a middle path between religion and atheism, or faith and logic. It is an understandable attempt to be open to things we don't know while rejecting the conviction of religion. Nevertheless, going into our practice as a "spiritual" person can create problems far bigger than those it solves in trying to find this middle way.

Part of what draws most of us to spirituality is, of course, *experience* as opposed to *belief*. At some point you may have had a spiritual experience, like a deeply blissful moment, a feeling of deep belonging, an overwhelming sense of love, a connection with the unspoken and nonlinear wisdom of nature, a non-dual view of being both the watcher and the watched, a deep immersion in emptiness (or fullness), and on and on.

The paradox is that a genuine spiritual experience always gives us a sense of a world beyond our limited ego view…and our ego immediately attempts to make that experience part of its view! This is a very *human* thing to do, so it's not a *bad* thing, or something to feel ashamed of doing, or something that's *stupid*. We *all* do it, in one way or another. And we all experience the problem this causes: When we try to possess a spiritual experience, we end

THE PROBLEM WITH A SPIRITUAL IDENTITY

up corrupting the experience while also making it impossible to transition from an *experience we have* to *something we live*. This is one of the main ways that we get stuck—trying to possess our spiritual experiences with our egos.

Centuries before there was Zen in Japan, there was Chan in China, and it laid the foundations for the Buddhism that would eventually spread to Tibet, Japan, and the West.[2] In the ninth Century, a great meditation master, Nanquan Puyan (c. 749 – c. 835), was asked by his student, "Master, what is the Way?"

He replied, "Ordinary mind is the way."

In the roughly 1,200 years since that famous reply was uttered, there has never been any serious disagreement from generations of Buddhist meditation masters that Puyan spoke a powerful truth. But how can *ordinary* mind be the way? What about the divine? What about enlightenment? What about Christ consciousness? What about holy books? Prayer? What about the non-dual, or emptiness? What about Gaia? What about ancestors and spirit guides and astrological conjunctions? What about other realms of existence, energy, chakras, past lives? *Ordinary mind is the way?* I must admit that it's hard to imagine selling many books or online courses with that slogan. Part of what we'll get up to in this book is to explore exactly why ordinary mind *is* the way, and exactly what that means for our own practice.

One problem with identifying as a spiritual person is that you attempt to possess your spiritual experiences, as I already stated. Another common problem is you may think that *only* spiritual experiences are legitimate and therefore try to destroy or get away from your petty thoughts and mental stories. In other words, meditation and spiritual practice become forms of attempting to kill the "bad" ego, and you think a busy mind means you're an unspiritual person. Jealousy, anger, lust, or shame may be unwelcomed and repressed because those are considered "lower" human emotions that are not enlightened or spiritual. As you will discover, this is a grave misunderstanding, and this view makes spiritual evolution impossible, causes

---

2 For geopolitical reasons, there is some controversy about whether Buddhism spread from China to Tibet, instead of from India to Tibet. The matter is not considered settled by academics.

repression of emotion and spiritual bypassing, and can deaden empathy and compassion both for self and for other.

A small but profound shift in perspective can begin the process of freeing you from being trapped by your ideas of what a "spiritual" person is, and therefore freeing you to experience things like awakening for yourself. This shift is actually quite simple, and I'll get into that in just a moment. But like so many simple things, it's far more profound and far more difficult to fully experience than it might seem. As long as you try to have and hold spiritual experiences for yourself, rather than let the experiences have and hold you, you will remain trapped in concepts of spirituality that cannot free you from yourself.

It's worth repeating: It's a very human thing to try to possess a spiritual experience. It's one of the *most* human things we can do. Beating yourself up for doing it doesn't help—and won't work. It's a hard habit to break, but when you do, the universe will open herself to you and share her secrets. We just can't keep what we find.

This book is designed as an invitation to view your spiritual experiences in a much simpler way. I know this is challenging when we have such beautifully sophisticated maps of our own spiritual selves that we've become quite attached to using. Zen has been pulling spiritual maps from people's hands for centuries, of course, but Zen has also been inexorably bound to Japanese imperial culture that can make it challenging for modern, Westernized minds. We'll use the tools of Zen, but we'll modernize them to be applicable to the world we find ourselves in today.

SPIRITUALITY DEFINED

Let's take a step back and define spirituality. I define it as the *search* for the *sacred*. I think this is a pretty good definition. By "search" I mean this is an ongoing journey, a process that begins with the discovery of something sacred hidden right here in the seemingly profane life of a modern human. By "sacred" I mean discovering a perspective that illuminates some kind of transcendence, immanence, boundlessness, or ultimacy.

But the key here is *insight*, not *belief*. It is often said in Zen, for instance, that, "you need to deepen your insight." This means go back to the meditation cushion, sit in meditation, and see if a deeper illumination can be allowed to arise within you.

If *belief* is the domain of religion, then *insight* is the domain of spirituality. The realization of a spiritual *insight* is more important than having a spiritual *belief*, in the same way the comprehension of a scientific *insight* is more important than having a scientific *belief*. It's great if you *believe* climate change is real, but really what good is that? You're merely parroting the insight of others; you have nothing to base it on but faith, and an educated climate skeptic will tear your pants off in an argument. It's far better if you've looked at the data and had the interior *illumination* that the scientific evidence *shows* that climate change is real. Not all of us have the time, inclination, intelligence, or energy to become experts in all the places we have opinions, which is why we tend to cite experts in the defense of our beliefs. And there's nothing wrong with looking at the majority of climate scientists, seeing that almost all of them think that climate change is real and is caused by human activity, and then saying, "Well, I think we should listen to the overwhelming majority of people whose job it is to think about these things." But we often defend our *beliefs* as if they were our *insights*. This is part of why the world is so much at war with itself.

Spiritual insight can't be taught but instead needs to be fully realized for oneself, the same way that love must be experienced in order to be fully understood. You can talk to a fourteen-year-old about love until you're blue in the face, but nothing you say will prepare them for the intensity of their first experience of falling in love with another person. The depth of the experience must be felt in one's being, not just understood as intellectual knowledge, in order to be fully comprehended. The same can be said of intense heartbreak, of the unexpected death of someone you love, of experiencing the pain of the last few breaths of an exhausted marriage, or any number of things that must be felt and not ever just understood.

Spiritual *insight* comes, in part, from being able to let go of the self—thoughts, feelings, stories, beliefs, etc. This doesn't mean that those who have done this are *egoless*, however—egoless is what an infant is, which is why they can't hold their heads up, pee their pants, and need to be fed to survive. Highly realized spiritual masters do not *identify* with their egos and their thoughts, stories, and feelings. Being *awakened* or *deeply realized* or *enlightened* means being radically dis-identified with the self and from identity of any kind. Yet the self and the identities are still very much there—they're just not held very tightly.

These rare people—and they are truly rare—certainly experience pain, but they experience a great deal less suffering because they're not in the habit of *resisting the world as it is*. Rain is wet, snow is cold, the sun is warm, life ends in death, heartache hurts, love is expansive, and many other things simply happen without reactivity.

Many of us take up meditation or prayer in order to find some degree of peace in the world, but for most of us the path is blocked even before we begin. We'll never move beyond a glimpse of freedom because we're in the way. Most meditations we learn are designed to give our egos something to do: We count our breaths, we focus on our inhales, we label our thoughts as thoughts and let them go, we come into our body in a particular way, we recite mantras, or we pray. These things are all fine, but they can't deliver us into liberation, into freedom, into the ability to *be with what is*. Meditations that give you nothing to do are simple, and in that simplicity they can be quite challenging.

This is meditation with a simple goal: to *allow* the clarity that is already *here* to arise (not *find* the clarity—finding is doing, which the ego loves, and awakening isn't *there* in some *other* place. It is *here, now*).

Allow the clarity that is already here to arise within you. That could be this entire book. Nothing about identity in that. No crystals or malas needed, no six-part course to take, no two-hour satsang, no week-long retreat, no divinity. If your experience includes a realization of a creator, that expression might be: *Allow the God-consciousness that is already here to arise within you.* God or no God, it makes no difference to the awakened Christian monks I've trained with, the agnostic Zen masters who I've studied under, or the mystical Tibetan lamas under whom I first took vows. God or no God is

THE PROBLEM WITH A SPIRITUAL IDENTITY

irrelevant to all of them because their spiritual insights are so deep that they transcend utterly such meaningless distinctions. (If you're saying to yourself, "Wait, God or no God is *meaningless*? How is that possible?" you're not crazy, or dull. But it's a truth that's rooted in spiritual *insight*, not in logic or learning or philosophy or ideas. And it should make a lot more sense to you, in your being, by the end of this book.)

Pure awareness, or God, or spirit, or suchness, or enlightenment—or whatever you want to call the Omega and the Alpha and the real goal of your meditation—*isn't responding to your meditations*. It's not affected by your meditation techniques, and it doesn't come and go. Your *ability* to sit as awareness itself is what comes and goes. Pure awareness, or God, or spirit, or suchness doesn't ever become *part of you*. God never becomes *a part of you* because God could never be apart from you. And you don't become part of it. Awakening is simply awake. God is simply God. God is simply awake. *You* can't wake up; you can't become enlightened because *you* can't keep what you find here. But you can *allow* what's already here and notice for yourself that awareness is aware, not you.

You can then discover, as we say in Zen, that you have everything you need and have been "awake" this entire time. That's why in Zen we say that teaching meditation is "selling water by the river," because you're teaching someone to find something that's right here, right now. The only real instruction is to show them what they already have.

Zen also calls enlightenment the "gateless gate" because once you have awakened, you look and see that awakening was here the entire time—you go through a gate only to see there was never a gate in the first place.

Allow the clarity that is already here to arise within you.

Those are easy words for me to say and might even be easy for you to understand with your mind. But knowing this in the depths of your being is another thing entirely, and something that we'll spend much of this book doing.

Most of us meditate not with a radical approach to allowing, but instead with a goal in mind, like relaxation or mindfulness or greater equanimity or, God help us, *enlightenment*. We think we need to do things like *quiet our mind*, or do visualization practices, or clarify our karma, or mature from spiritual adolescents to spiritual adults to spiritual elders, or 10,000 other things that keep us from the truth.

If you're looking to spiritually *awaken*, really awaken out of the dream of your separate self, you need to stop the practices that have your ego looking to perfect your practice, gain powerful "spiritual" insights, uncover "powerful" methods, or be seen as some kind of holder of wisdom.

The good news is that when you actually do nothing with your mind and leave your ego alone, you can find this sense of being "awake" inside of yourself—a luminescent core of your being that is already perfectly still, already perfectly awake, already perfectly enlightened, already fully in love with the world as it is, and that already has everything it needs. *But you can't have it for yourself.* You can't keep all your judgments about the world, your sense of being *so fucking right* about this or that. The practice is to get out of the way in order to know this truth for yourself, which will also shatter your *self.*

The great teachers have told us, over and over again, that enlightenment isn't really spiritual at all. That word *enlightenment* has been bastardized, spiritualized, and miscategorized, yet isn't complicated. Enlightenment includes *everything*. And by everything, they mean *everything*, not everything *except* Donald Trump, leaf blowers, the patriarchy, a cold swimsuit sticking to your thigh on a chilly night, rush hour traffic, and that asshole you dated last year.

As we'll see in this chapter, this truth is really a problem for most spiritual people. Because if we're in love with half the world but hate the other half, how do we ever get our mind into a place where we can accept that the deepest spiritual insight that we can have not only isn't spiritual, but it includes everything in the manifest universe—including all the nasty bits?

Enlightenment is intimacy with all things.[3]—*Zen Master Dogen*

---

[3] This is sometimes interpreted as "…intimacy with the 10,000 things," which is saying the same thing.

THE PROBLEM WITH A SPIRITUAL IDENTITY

And by "all things," Zen Master Dogen means *all* things, not just "most things," "the spiritual things," "the good things," "the liberal things," "the free market things," or "the moral things."

The enlightened mind doesn't condone the "bad" things, mind you. But it also doesn't condemn them either. It just accepts that they're *real*, for now. Just like we're real, for now. Until we're not. (If you feel a tripwire of an ethical dilemma here, you're onto something, but I'll hold that off until Chapter 8, where together we'll plug it into some of the simplicity, and complexity, we'll discover along the way.)

Enlightenment isn't spiritual, yet all spirituality flows from it. At the core of your being is tremendous peace, and love, and equanimity. Not as thoughts, beliefs, or things to be cultivated…or that even *can be* cultivated. And they're not *better* than their opposites. They're just *truths* that arise out of the pure essence of who you are. They're more *interesting* than their opposites because they arise out of your direct experience of the very deepest part of your nature, our nature, my nature. And you can find them and see them for yourself.

In this book I'll do my best to highlight how you too can *allow* this to be. You may, however, have to leave behind your ideas about spirituality, about the world, about God, about the nature of the universe, and about enlightenment, because none of those ideas will help you discover this truth for yourself.

WHY DO YOU HAVE A SPIRITUAL PRACTICE?

Let us start, then, at the beginning, with the asking of a simple question: Why do you have a spiritual practice in the first place?

There are many good answers to this question, but my favorite context for this comes from my own teacher, the fiery and sometimes ornery Junpo Denis Kelly Roshi, the eighty-third patriarch in Rinzai Zen. Junpo was my teacher and my friend, and we wrote two books together before he passed in the spring of 2021.[4]

---

4 Keith Martin-Smith, *A Heart Blown Open: The Life and Practice of Junpo Denis Kelly Roshi* (Divine Arts Media, 2012); Junpo Denis Kelly Roshi and Keith Martin-Smith, *The Heart of Zen* (Berkeley, CA: North Atlantic Books, 2014).

Awakened mind (enlightenment) cannot be disturbed. Nothing but you can move you out of stable clear awareness and presence and into contraction—nothing. If you have a spiritual practice or belief that isn't strong enough to withstand prison, the death of a loved one, infidelity, bankruptcy, or the diagnosis of a terminal illness—it may be time to start over.

If your consciousness cannot remain undisturbed by these things—which doesn't mean no tears or no emotions, by the way—you might want to ask what is missing in your practice, and why you're bothering in the first place.[5]

A spiritual practice can be about many things, but a deep approach with the correct frame can offer nothing less than liberation. The spiritual teacher Adyashanti used to frequently ask his students, "What do you want *more than anything else*?" Some would find themselves, with a bit of digging, saying they wanted the *truth*—the real truth. And he would always then ask them, "Do you want the truth, or do you want to be special? Because you can't have both."

If you're going to bother with a spiritual practice at all, you might as well strive for the truth, or to awaken fully from your egoic dream, because anything less than that will leave you, as Junpo said, unable to withstand what life will inevitably throw your way. Your practice will be hollow at the core because of a belief that you're somehow special in how you do it, or who you are, or in what you gain. This is the making of your spiritual identity, which is the making of a trap from which you can't escape.

A spiritual *identity*, you see, might be a better and more helpful identity in stressful times than that of, say, a banker, but not necessarily (and probably not in a financial crisis). But more times than not, when the shit really hits the fan, our spiritual identity is just another thought form, another set of beliefs fueled by the ways we string together our musings to create stories and thereby our worlds.

Beliefs aren't much comfort against the seeming chaos of life, or we'd all just have great beliefs that insulated us fully from the suffering of the world. But we don't. At the first sign of trouble our spiritual beliefs are often out the

---

5 Junpo Denis Kelly Roshi and Keith Martin-Smith, *The Heart of Zen: Enlightenment, Emotional Maturity, and What It Really Takes for Spiritual Liberation* (Berkeley, CA: North Atlantic Books, 2014).

THE PROBLEM WITH A SPIRITUAL IDENTITY

door, leaving us to deal with the mess of life without all those understandings we thought would be so comforting.

Our identity is created by our thoughts experienced over time. We can have incredibly complex identities based on the tension or lack of tension between our internal experience and our cultural one. (Some of these identities are now considered marginalized, but oddly can be simple semantic choices. For instance, someone raised male, straight, white, and middle class can choose to be *queer*—without changing anything else about their life—and become part of a marginalized group. This isn't to minimize or marginalize the struggles that queer people face, but merely to show how fluid and powerful identity has become in our culture.)

The larger point, however, is that our culture is at an inflection point as it wakes up to both the liberations and limitations of intersectional identities: How do ethnicities, histories, power differentials, implicit or explicit cultural biases, and other dimensions generate new self-meanings and ways of interpreting who we hold ourselves to be? We will explore identity more later in this book, but for now let's peel back a few layers on something most of us take for granted: *who we think we are.*

From a Zen perspective we look at things a little differently, making a distinction between the relative and the absolute (although that distinction too eventually falls away). All thinking is relative, meaning thoughts are not permanent. They arise, they exist for a time, they vanish. Any egoic identity is created by our impermanent thoughts experienced over time, creating an impermanent identity. We can all think of identities we've let go: maybe a counterculture teenage punk, a responsible wife, an angry rebel, a liberal activist, a nice guy, a conservative, a slut or a prude, a man or woman (if someone transitions to the opposite), a gender identity of any kind, etc. Other identities are fixed, such as ones based on our physical appearance (people of color can't choose to be white), but they too vanish as death takes them from us.

Death comes equally to us all, and makes us all equal when it comes.
—*John Donne*

While an identity can be useful and very much necessary to navigate life and to grow up parts of ourselves, it can be a double-edged sword when it comes to having and sustaining spiritual experiences that happen beyond its reach. You might have a good objection as to why your identity is very necessary and very real. And your identity *is* real—it's just not fixed or permanent or, as you will see, very stable.

Maybe you fought hard to find this part of yourself, the "truest" version of you (so far). Maybe you feel your identity is under attack, and claiming it positions you as an activist and ally. Perhaps it's something you've never really questioned, but it feels so obviously true and natural that you can't really imagine life without it. Perhaps you think that letting go of an identity is itself an act of privilege that abandons those who don't have that option. Or that letting it go will plunge you into madness. There are so many reasons to have and to hold an identity, and it's not my place to tell you how you should or shouldn't hold yours. But I can speak to how that identity intersects with your spirituality, and how you can have your identity but paradoxically be less attached to it, which isn't to deny its existence but to honor its limitations and its transparent impermanence.

If we look a little closer, we see that any self-identity has to be made up of how we view ourselves. This view will likely be reinforced by society, positively or negatively. But at its core, identity is made up of thought. And our thoughts are a fascinating place to bring some attention, some awareness. While we can harness our thoughts into practical thinking, on occasion, we are utterly powerless to stop them. And we cannot really control *what* we're thinking most of the time, either. If we could, we'd simply choose not to focus on our last breakup, or our mortality, or our sick child, or our test tomorrow, or whatever might be bothering us. Perhaps we'd only ever think spiritual thoughts, never have thoughts that upset us, or never have thoughts that end up hurting ourselves or hurting someone else when they're acted on. We'd be the sovereign of our own minds. But we know that's not true and, on the whole, we feel much more like the slave to our thoughts, beliefs, feelings, and yes, identity—spiritual and otherwise.

THE PROBLEM WITH A SPIRITUAL IDENTITY

Said another way: If we can't find freedom and lasting peace with our thinking minds, how can an identity built on those thoughts and feelings help us achieve freedom and lasting peace? They can't, and on some level we all know this already because we've already tried it, time and time again, throughout our entire lives. Most of us are trying it even now. Ask yourself: What identity are you searching for right now? Perhaps even the one motivating you to read this book?

Sometimes in deep meditation, or just for some spontaneous and unknown reason, we can pop out of our thinking mind entirely and find ourselves in a place where we are simply looking out at the world, and at ourselves, as everything arises. In those moments, we might experience our thoughts and our entire identity as arising within a much greater awareness, no different than how the wind arises out of nothing and dashes across our skin, coming from nothing and going into nothing. And yet even without thinking and without any externally defined identity, there is awareness simply and powerfully looking out at all that is. These moments of grace, of liberation, can completely change our world…so long as we don't try to hold onto them. And they have nothing whatsoever to do with a spiritual identity.

If you're convinced that you're in control of your thoughts, then simply set a timer for two minutes and choose to not think. It's unlikely you'll make it past twenty seconds before a few thoughts arise, and by the one-minute mark whole ideas should be streaming past.

The reason you can't stop your thoughts is simple: *You are not thinking, you are being thought.* I know. It sounds like something a clever spiritual person would say. But it's the same with our breath: We can control our breath when we choose to, but most of the time breathing happens to us. We can't stop our breath because we're not breathing, either. We're being breathed.

Now, these are just words on a page or sounds entering your ears. They mean nothing until you experience their truth for yourself. But one of the goals of this book is that you may, soon, experience the profound sensation of *being thought*, and the incredibly powerful sensation of *being breathed*. I assure you that if you've never experienced this, the experience will transcend anything you might imagine.

There's one final point I'd like to drive home. I am not saying you shouldn't have an identity—absurd (especially since society may have expectations about your identity that require your attention, care, and action if you're in a non-privileged position). Thoughts and identities are quite useful, and they're indispensable to the business of being a human being. But it's good to keep in mind that your identity, no matter how profound or brilliant or original or righteous or historically oppressed, cannot liberate you from your suffering.

THE ROOT OF THE PROBLEM

Identities are vital to the business of being human. We must all create and sustain identities—our stories of ourselves—as we differentiate from our family of origin and, for some of us, our culture. For most of us, that's enough—creating an identity that is our own and is more or less aware of its history, its culture, its enculturation, and its biases and neurotic conditioning. (Those last two are very good things to be aware of.) But some of us will be called to move beyond identity and into something less defined, including moving beyond an identity as a spiritual person or a spiritual teacher. In this place, our identity is something that is more situation-specific. For example: When I teach, I'm a teacher. When I write, I'm a writer. When I meditate, I'm a meditator. When I do martial arts, I'm a martial artist. Those identities arise as necessary to serve a function, but they're not something that I hold inside of me as some indelible part of my being. When I'm walking in the park, watching the sunset, or watching football, I'm none of those things.

A spiritual identity is unique because in some way or another it is trying to find a reality deeper than the one in which it currently finds itself. Typically, spiritual people will share a good deal of these beliefs about the world:

THE PROBLEM WITH A SPIRITUAL IDENTITY

- kindness over aggression
- love over indifference or hate
- anti-racism over racism
- equanimity over anger
- feminine over masculine
- spiritual over materialistic
- environmentalism over capitalism
- action over inaction
- natural over manmade
- spirit over matter
- soul over ego
- peace over war
- liberal over conservative
- being over doing
- transcendent over worldly
- embodied over analytical
- quiet over noisy
- inclusive over hierarchical

Now there's nothing wrong with wanting a more peaceful, kind, just, and fair society where more people are aware of the impact of mindless consumption, unconscious power structures, and their behavior on the larger world. These are noble and powerful goals to have and to work toward.

It becomes problematic, however, when we take these ideas into our spiritual practices. The problems arise not because we want to make the world a better place. To state the obvious: It's okay to want to make the world a better place, but it's also much more complicated than that. We assume, as "spiritual" people, that we would all agree on what it means to make the world a better place. But many of the most diabolical dictators in history, and the most abusive cult leaders, were convinced they too were doing exactly that. There is nothing inheritably ennobling or clarifying about wanting to improve the world *as we see fit*, because that goal, like so many that seem good and just, can get hijacked by our nastier, unconscious parts.

Take another look at that list of typical spiritual beliefs. Most of us will think half of that list is better than the other half. If we could stop there, we might still be able to bring true clarity into our spiritual practice, but almost none of us stop there. If we really tell the truth, it's far more accurate to say that the half we like has *more reason to exist* than the half we don't—and that we should *exterminate* patriarchy, *abolish* capitalism, and be *intolerant* of the intolerant. That sets us up into an odd place of not accepting the world *as it is* in our spiritual practice or in society at large.

I want to slow this way, way down, because it's very easy to misunderstand this point. I'm *not* saying you should *accept, support,* or *ignore* that which needs your attention. I'm *not* saying you need to *ignore* the environmental issues facing us, or *accept* child sex trafficking as "just the way things are," or *support* corrupted systems like that of American prisons. Junpo used to say, "Cynicism, denial, and apathy are not helpful traits on the spiritual path." So I'm not saying watch the world burn from a Zen haze because "it's all real, man." I am saying that the universe gives precisely zero fucks if *you accept it as it is or not*—reality just goes on being real, in the same way a rainy day goes on raining regardless of your opinion of the rain.

This is a problem with a spiritual identity: It prefers "spiritual" things, like nonviolence over violence. Or environmental sustainability over capitalistic industry. As a citizen, an activist, or a concerned human being, there is nothing wrong with having these preferences and in fighting for them. I'm certainly not suggesting we allow rampant corporate control of our government or systemic racism to continue, or that there is something wrong with being in opposition to those things and fighting to remove them as much as possible from our culture. As a spiritual practitioner, however, believing that one half of the world (the half you like) *has more reason to exist* than the other half of the world (the half you don't like) is hugely problematic, because that thing continues to exist *no matter how you feel about it.* The world, you see, is not divided. Only we are, and *only we* project that division outwards where it doesn't exist.

In other words, reality is not divided by its very nature, and it's not in opposition to any part of itself. We are divided in all the ways explained so far—we love some things and hate others, we think we're right about this and others wrong about that, we bristle at a world that isn't more in tune with how we think it should be. And we project that perceived division onto the world, onto that undivided reality, where it simply does not exist. At its core, the universe is whole and undivided and complete, and therefore so are *you*, no matter what your opinion of things might be.

Remember: You cannot be liberated and opinioned at the same time. And since we're telling the truth, in our highly politicized times most of

THE PROBLEM WITH A SPIRITUAL IDENTITY

us don't stop with wanting to get *rid of* the half of the world we don't like. Truthfully, we want to *eradicate* those parts, a strategy that creates *tremendous* internal opposition to the world *as it is*.

Well, you say: So fucking what? Why shouldn't I be in utter opposition to things that I know are harmful, destructive, toxic, and otherwise unfit to exist? Because the deepest spiritual insights we can have as a human being are not shrouded in our preferences, biases, or opinions. We can't be liberated and opinioned at the same time. Those are mutually exclusive states, like awake and asleep, sober and drunk, alive and dead, and wise and foolish. When we're at war with part of the world, we are always at war with a part of ourselves, and if we're at war with ourselves, we cannot be free. (And freedom, as we'll discover, is only the beginning of the spiritual journey. There are so many more interesting treasures to behold on the path of awakening than our supposed freedom.) There can be no genuine spiritual insight that refuses to accept reality as it is. That's just a belief that is looking out onto the world and saying "*that* deserves to exist but *that* doesn't" as the universe goes on arising, not caring at all how much you don't like parts of it.

There is a Taoist story of an old farmer who had worked his crops for many years. One day his horse ran away. Upon hearing the news, his neighbors came to visit. "Such bad luck," they said sympathetically.

"Maybe," the farmer replied. The next morning the horse returned, bringing with it three other wild horses. "How wonderful," the neighbors exclaimed.

"Maybe," replied the old man. The following day, his son tried to ride one of the untamed horses, was thrown, and broke his leg.

The neighbors again came to offer their sympathy on his misfortune. "Maybe," answered the farmer. The day after, military officials came to the village to draft young men into the army. Seeing that the son's leg was broken, they passed him by.

The neighbors congratulated the farmer on how well things had turned out. "Maybe," said the farmer.

To state it just once more for emphasis: Acceptance of things as they are doesn't mean we have to let polluters pollute, racists run police departments, despots run countries, and rapists rape. That is not at all what this means. When we look out at the world from an awakening state, we're simply not at war with what we see there already existing—and we're not at war with those parts of ourselves that refuse to accept it. We accept the world as it is even as we work to change it, and even as our hearts break open at the suffering we encounter.

I am not offering a ticket to watching the world burn from a place of enlightened detachment, from the Zen student's cool and detached persona. No, the pain of the world's ignorance and of the host of man-made problems can become very, very intense and very, very intimate. You may find yourself weeping at the sight of a tree being cut down. Or in tears at the sight of a piece of plastic on the beach. There are more tears in seeing how things really are, not less; more times you are literally brought to your knees by seeing reality as it is, not less. This is because you're willing to see the world without bracing yourself against the parts you don't like or don't think should exist. My teacher, Junpo, judged the depth of others' awakening not by their spiritual insight but by the depth of their compassion.

The depth of our compassion is a marker of our spiritual depth. This is not the depth of our pity, which is looking at something and shaking our head saying, "So sad," as you move on with your life. Spiritual insight is not measured by the depth of one's outrage, which might simply be a refusal to accept what is. No, compassion for the pain of the world as it is now will take you to your knees as your heart breaks—without having to turn away from it in judgment and contraction, in anger and disbelief, in numbness or fatigue, or in a righteous rage. When you're one with the world, you're one with the world's pain.

One final point that is important to make: We do not ever need to get rid of identities, spiritual or otherwise. We need our egos, even as fully awakened beings. Far too many spiritual seekers go to war with their own minds and try to destroy their egos, along with their less spiritual thoughts and ways of being, ensuring they will never know true wisdom and never have lasting peace. When the mind goes to war with itself, the war never ends.

DIVIDED AND CONQUERED

When we refuse to accept certain parts of reality or hate their existence, part of each one of us can get pushed into psychological shadow. This is a pretty obvious phenomenon when say, a group of frat guys beat up a kid for being gay. While there are certainly cultural beliefs, peer pressuring, socioeconomic factors, and educational levels at play, studies have also found another consistent reason: Homophobic people often have unacknowledged feelings of attraction toward the same gender.[6] Put another way, their own homoerotic feelings are in shadow and they hate those feelings in themselves. When they see someone manifesting those feelings, they pounce.

Yet this phenomenon can be harder and more insidious to spot when it's something that seems virtuous. Black Studies professor Ibram X. Kendi has pointed out that until we—black, white, and other—claim and identify the racist parts of ourselves, we are terribly ineffective at finding helpful ways to bring more awareness to racist policies, ideas, and narratives. He maintains that racism is more like a state of mind than a trait, so that we could be racist in one moment and antiracist in the next, depending on how we're thinking and acting.

What is the danger of being at war with some part of the world, even something as horrible as racism? Well, if we haven't faced up to the inner racist inside of us, then that *unconscious racism* can wreak havoc on our conscious decision making. Kendi's word for freeing ourselves from this is *antiracist*, which is stronger than *not racist* because it implies one is working against not only what they see in the world but also what they see inside of themselves. An antiracist, by Kendi's definition, accepts the world as it is

---

6 https://psycnet.apa.org/record/2012-02599-001

now and works inside of that acceptance to create different behaviors the only place they matter: in the moment.[7]

When we hate something out in the world and refuse to accept it might be inside of us, too, we can strive to stamp it out of everything and everyone in a fit of zealotry. Nazis are a good example here, because if ever there was an epitome of evil, it's them. No one comes to the defense of Nazis or Nazism (except those already on the fringes of society).

Nazis are a pretty safe place to heap one's scorn and hatred, for they believed in the racial superiority of the Aryan race (despite it not actually being a race). If you don't think *you* have the capacity to be a Nazi somewhere inside of you, you are far more likely to become a zealot. True, you might not goosestep to your next Pilates class, but you might lose the capacity to see why antifascists, with their covered faces and quick move toward violence, look an awful lot like the people they're supposed to be fighting (namely, *fascists*). To remind those whose memory of history may be a bit faint: Fascists are those who put race and nation ahead of any individuality and support that form of society by force through a strong dictatorial power.

This can be hard for liberal folks to see because the antifas are on *their* side and seem to be fighting against, in the United States at least as of the writing of this book, Trumpism and racism. It's also likely true that many on the left have disowned their own inner *fascists*. A fascist would have *an intolerance of those unlike themselves and a desire to rid the country of those kinds of people*. And yet some on the left have become utterly intolerant of those unlike themselves. They start with a rejection of what was once a liberal value, tolerance. And as we can all too easily see, this is how one starts a war, not how one creates lasting peace.

Liberals understandably see the problems of racism, sexism, and other social problems and want to eradicate them, and yet this seemingly noble stance can be problematic. For we must see these things inside of ourselves and begin there—not with an iron fist of intolerance at what we find, but

---

7 Ibram X. Kendi, *How to Be an Antiracist* (New York: One World, 2019

THE PROBLEM WITH A SPIRITUAL IDENTITY

with a velvet glove of understanding and inner dialog. Only then can we help others to make this transition.

Both liberals and conservatives of all stripes might do well to listen to Aleksandr Isayevich Solzhenitsyn. This Russian, Nobel Prize–winning novelist and philosopher spoke out against the Soviet Union and Communism through a deeply humanistic lens. He refused to see those who had exiled him and his family, and ruined his homeland, as merely "evil."

> *If only it were all so simple. If only there were evil people somewhere insidiously committing evil deeds, and it were necessary only to separate them from the rest of us and destroy them. But the line dividing good and evil cuts through the heart of every human being. And who is willing to destroy a piece of his own heart?*[8]—Aleksandr Solzhenitsyn

There's nothing wrong with wanting to educate people and reform our various systems of education and law to better accommodate and address injustices we see in the world. There is a problem with wanting to *eradicate* certain kinds of people or even certain kinds of ideas, rather than wanting to *transform* them.

Ordinary mind is the way. Enlightenment is intimacy with all things. As awakened beings, we do not reject the bad things in the world, nor do we resist them. Rape, war, discrimination, poverty, sex trafficking, and worse are all real and all happening now. We don't close our hearts to these things or turn away with "compassion fatigue." We accept these things are real, for now, just like you and I are real, for now. We don't hate or resist what is, any more than we hate and resist the entire winter because we don't like the cold, or hate and resist life because we're afraid of death.

This doesn't mean we do nothing. It most definitely doesn't mean we feel nothing. My teacher Junpo tells a story of seeing a tree freshly cut down and the sap oozing from it, and falling to his knees in tears as the tree "bled"

---

8 *The Gulag Archipelago*, Harper Perennial Modern Classics; Abridged edition, 2007

to death in front of him. He was one with the sentience around him, and it broke his heart wide open. That experience also was part of what drove him to become a lifelong environmentalist. The Dalai Lama talks of, when he was a young boy, seeing a group of other boys stone a puppy to death, and he has used that memory to open his heart to compassion and love and openness to the world, to those boys, and to the puppy.

Accepting the world as it is doesn't mean doing so with a smile, although truthfully you may find yourself smiling a great deal more often when you're no longer at war with what is.

CHAPTER 2

What Is Spiritual, Anyway?

Just past my sixteenth birthday I began having spontaneous "spiritual" experiences that I had neither cultivated nor desired, things that came on like a sudden sneeze and were about as welcome. We might call these "state" experiences in that they seemed to happen "outside" of my day-to-day ego view, in what can be called non-ordinary states of consciousness. It's called a "state" because it comes and goes and is not fixed the way your egoic view of the world is more-or-less fixed; as such, it can feel and be very disruptive.

This was in the mythical late 1980s, a time of wondrous mullets, fantastically subversive music that existed underneath all the fantastically awful music, Ronald Regan and Max Headroom, NWA and Rick Ashley, and of course the high-water mark for the now irrelevant MTV.

I wasn't a spiritually inclined kid, nor was I ever religious. Earlier, when I was thirteen, the idea of Christ and God simply perplexed me, and as I grew into my early teens I took up the mantel of atheism. This was greatly aided by my religious teachers, who were unable to offer a rational or even slightly cogent defense of their faith, and who preferred mindless discipline and dogma over curiosity and intellectual stimulation. The solution they offered to curious young minds was simple: Don't ask such difficult questions and do as you're told. This kind of instruction didn't work for me even at that young age.

And so there I was a few years later, not far past my sixteenth birthday, walking the family dog on a beautiful fall evening, a harvest moon glowing through fast-moving clouds that punctuated an otherwise clear sky. Like many sixteen-year-olds, my life was a confusing mix of differentiation from my family, a newfound and very unstable sense of self, longing for a particular girl who I was terrified to approach, and through it all a massive insecurity that ran through me about everything from the quality of my skin to the depth of my intelligence.

I was looking up at the moon and noticing the beauty of her fullness when I was suddenly, viscerally, connected to all of humanity, past and present, as a living reality. It was the recognition, in the depth of my bones, that I was part of every human who had ever lived and they were a part of me. It wasn't a thought or a feeling (there is nothing terribly profound about the thought *I am connected to all humans past and present and future*), but was more of an *experience*. It was something that transcended thought utterly—the young atheist found himself having an experience that lifted his heart into laugher, brought a smile to his face, and made the world inarguably interconnected, whole, wholesome, and perfect as it was. The experience was, in part, the realization that the intense loneliness that I lived with day-to-day was inconceivable from this place, for I was connected to every human being who'd ever looked up at the brightness of the moon and contemplated her beauty.

I cried out—I literally cried out—with laughter and with the joy of seeing how much bigger the world, and I, were. The bliss I felt was unlike any joy I'd ever encountered up to that point in my life. It was like my heart sang for the very first time, and I was freer than I'd ever been. The intensity, the immediacy of the experience faded within a few minutes, but the effects stayed with me for hours. I marveled at the profundity of my own existence, at my own capacity to be aware that I was aware. I finished the walking of the dog, did some homework, and, before I went to bed, looked out a window at that full moon like she was a lover. I went to bed alive and happy.

WHAT IS SPIRITUAL, ANYWAY?

I woke up me. Which is to say angry, confused, and unhappy. I was a sullen teenager again, one who didn't particularly enjoy his home life, his school, his appearance, his car (such as it was), his chronic single status, or pretty much anything else. Yet now I had this odd memory, this thing lodged into my consciousness, this experience that defied explanation. My Catholic educators didn't teach me the mystical works of the Romantic poets like Wordsworth or Keats, nor the spiritual longings of Rilke and Elliot, nor the numinous ideas of the great Sufi poets. These were all men so in love with God and so alive to the kinds of experiences that I had just had that they spent their lives finding the language for the indescribable. Yet they were alien to me.

Our conscious mind cannot be greater than the things we have known (or, in the more poetic words of Pink Floyd, *"And all you touch/And all you see/Is all your life will ever be."*[9]) I had no reference point for anything mystical and no sense that such a thing was possible. Mysticism didn't exist for me because at sixteen I'd never heard of it. The best my young atheist mind could make of it was some circuits had crossed in my brain and given me a pleasant but illusory few hours of bliss. I tried to dismiss the experience as a one-off odd event. And yet that splinter remained, the experience of a world whole and undivided that I could not, as hard as I tried, dismiss utterly.

A few years later I was standing in my parents' driveway. I was now a complicated twenty-year-old who was deeply questioning everything, including the nature of reality and my own existence. I devoured books on science and philosophy, yet still had never heard or encountered anything mystical in any writings. Based on my singularly negative experience of Catholicism, my interests in books and classes reflected a growing skepticism toward anything supernatural, and I was unable to make a distinction between religion and spirituality or mysticism and faith. All were equally ridiculous to my young mind, a sad attempt to overcome the hard and adult

---

9 "Breathe," track 1 on Pink Floyd, *The Dark Side of the Moon*, Harvest Records, 1973.

truth that life had no meaning, and that what meaning we found we generated arbitrarily.

I closed the door to my car and glanced up at the stars. Then, just like before, I had a bit of a spiritual sneeze, but a much, much bigger one. One moment I was standing in the driveway and the next I *was* the stars. And I was *me* looking at *them* at the same time I was *the stars* being looked at. My identity was everywhere, and nowhere. I was the car. The driveway. My right shoe. The dog shit in the yard. All things and no things—just awareness itself, and awareness was everywhere and everything. How inadequate those words are to explain the experience! But it was *absolute* in that no part of my egoic self remained. It was like Keith had been obliterated and yet awareness remained, awareness that was at once looking at the thing being looked at.

And the feeling—oh the feeling. It felt so fantastically fucking *awesome* that I again burst out laughing, but in a different way: I saw my tiny and existential twenty-year-old self was an object in an infinitely vast awareness, and in that awareness the smallness of my normal consciousness was so insignificant that it was simply hysterical. Life was a joke, and I was the punch-line, and it was *funny*. Side-splittingly funny. My dramas, fears, self-stories, and contractions were so irrelevant and so tiny that it was very funny that some tiny human named *Keith* took them with such grave seriousness. Everything I'd learned to that point at the university was also laughably irrelevant. In that space, there were no questions, no need to understand the universe, life and death, disease, war—it all made perfect sense by virtue of its existence, and my mind went as silent as a snow-filled field late at night.

Like the first experience, I went to bed that night liberated and I awoke imprisoned, the freedom of the previous night only a memory. And like before, I told no one about my experience, for in the light of day I had a terribly sobering thought: *What if this was sign of madness?* I had long ago decided that all the prophets were schizophrenics and yet there I was, having some kind of imaginary *thing* happening to me. If I wasn't careful, I thought, I might end up spouting some kind of mystical nonsense and moving in with a cult.

WHAT IS SPIRITUAL, ANYWAY?

These experiences kept happening. Many times they were like what I described above, what I would now call a non-dual experience of being both subject and object at the same time. Yet there were other, equally intoxicating states of being, not as liberating, but they were powerful proof that I was accessing a way of seeing the world that most people had never imagined, much less experienced. I'll give three more, brief examples for a sense of what my life was like back then.

Not long after my twenty-first birthday, I was having a beer with my cousin in a local bar and probably talking about a TV show when the most curious sensation came over me. My body went completely and utterly still. My entire system went quiet, like I'd been standing on vibrating ground *my entire life* and it just stopped. Which isn't the same as turned *off*. Everything was working as it always did: I was still talking to my cousin, still sipping my beer, still present in what was happening in the bar. But everything in my world had gone still. This time there was no bliss or laughter, just a kind of curiosity and an amazement as this stillness was so pervasive and powerful that I could almost see reality coming into existence, moment to moment. Over a few hours it too faded, but like all the other experiences it left a piece of itself behind, a bookmark that it might be possible to live in a different world than most people did.

A few years later, living in the East Village of New York as a young and struggling writer, I was stepping down a small, three-inch step between two parts of my 200-square-foot studio. As my right foot began to come down, my consciousness blew up out of my own head and in a microsecond was the literal cosmos, the entirety of the physical universe. And a millionth of a microsecond later I came contracting back down through the universe, across the expanse of space, into our solar system, down through the earth's atmosphere and the island of Manhattan, and crashed back into my own head. And my foot touched the ground. The entire trip had only taken the time it takes to step down a very small step, yet I had been gone for minutes it seemed, not a microsecond. I was left looking back out of my own, tiny eyes at my own, tiny apartment, confused and more than a little freaked out.

What the fuck was that all about? were the first thoughts that tumbled through my astonished mind.

I mentioned earlier that I never really understood the idea of Christ or of God, even as a child. I always saw the garish and often ghoulish corpse of Christ hanging from his wooden cross and felt only confusion. I was about twenty-three when a friend was married in my Philly neighborhood of Manayunk, in a beautiful large Catholic church there. There was a striking, life-sized carving of Christ inside. Looking at the artist's depiction of a handsome but saddened face, my heart opened to an overpowering love of everyone and everything. This wasn't a feeling of bliss or of wonderment, but a feeling of the infinite vastness of the heart and its ability to feel the suffering of everything and everyone in the world, without getting overwhelmed by it all.

I had to fight to keep from being taken to my knees in a public space with a rough and rowdy group of Philadelphians. In that intense moment, I was forever changed: All of Christianity suddenly made perfect sense. Not the dogma-infused rules and regulations of my childhood and adolescence, or the terrible corporal punishment I endured from priests and brothers of the Holy Cross, but the fire of Christos, the fire of divine love that burns brighter than a thousand suns and is limitless in its depth and its love. And like the other experiences, I was simply deposited back into my life—confused, shaken, bigger but less certain, and increasingly unsure of what was real.

These kinds of experiences just kept happening. I didn't meditate. I didn't pray, much less believe in a creator. I didn't burn incense, chant, or own a single crystal. I didn't listen to New Age CDs, read Ram Dass books, know anything whatsoever about Buddhism, or consider myself spiritual in the least. I was endlessly curious about existence and about my own consciousness, which continued to be a marvel. But mostly I read fiction and science books. Nothing in my world said that anyone anywhere had ever experienced the things I was experiencing, and so I slowly came to a conclusion: I was mentally ill.

Since I believed the prophets were madmen in a time before psychology and the angels and demons they saw projections of their own, distorted consciousness, I had to apply the same assessment to myself. This was the terrifying thought that came to dominate my day-to-day life. The only time that thought, the worry, wasn't with me, was when I was swept up in some kind of spontaneous mystical awakening.

My day-to-day world grew dark and frightening. I began to drink to keep the experiences repressed and quiet, setting up a problematic relationship with alcohol that would follow me for much of my adult life. I started having panic attacks on a regular basis. I had trouble holding down steady work. I hid all of these things from my friends, from the woman who would become my wife, from my parents, from my brother, from my best friend. I was scared, depressed, and alone. Utterly alone.

Except when I was connected to everyone and everything.

It made no fucking sense whatsoever.

But…before I finish this narrative, and with the hindsight offered by decades of living, learning, therapy, and practicing meditation, I now can tell you what was happening to me.

CONSCIOUSNESS DEFINED

Our consciousness includes our ego, of course. But it also includes much more, such as our unconscious conditioning and drives. Consciousness is that which is aware of things, including awareness of the ego itself. Right now, you know you're self-aware, and right now you know (or you should know) that your childhood, place of birth, education, race, gender, intelligence, wealth, and many other things have helped to shape who you are, in ways profound and mundane. And you probably know that your consciousness is a changing and fluid thing. One day you wake up in a terrible mood, and on the drive to work another driver suddenly cuts you off. And you scream a litany of curse words at that person, listen to the news on the radio, and wonder how the world ever got so totally fucked up. The sky seems dark and gray and you wonder whether there is any real point to life.

A few days later, you wake up in a great mood. And when someone cuts you off on your morning commute, you laugh at how rushed and inattentive he seemed. The news goes on and on, being the news, but you notice some good things happening in the world. The sun is low but bright as you drive, and you look forward to a dinner you're planning over the weekend with some friends. Life seems pretty good.

In both scenarios, your consciousness hugely influences how you experience reality. Nothing was objectively different—reality was pretty much the same on both of those days—and yet your experience of reality was completely dissimilar on those days. Our consciousness is the lens through which we filter life.

Consciousness is fluid and changing. It can be hugely expansive, like many people report after the birth of their first child, or while sitting bedside as a loved one passes. Our consciousness is hugely influenced by our brain chemistry, our personal psychology, our culture, and our physical surroundings (a war-torn city versus a quiet suburb versus the deck of a sailboat).

We think our consciousness is steady and stable, but of course it's not. Your consciousness at age two is very different from your consciousness when you're eighteen, and the consciousness of a wise sage is very different from that of a cutthroat Wall Street hedge fund manager. But how can we think of this in a spiritual sense, or when we're practicing meditation?

Consciousness is always in relationship to something, even if it's just in relationship to itself. That is a defining characteristic of consciousness, of ego, of self: relationship. Yours might be in relationship to God, or to yourself, or to your memories, or to the magic and mysteries of nature, or to the spiritual realm, or to other humans. If you're on a walk and contemplating your life, your consciousness is relating to itself, as well as to its stories, memories, relationships, desires, and many other things that will rise up and fall away. Distracted. Horny. Satisfied. Expansive. Curious. Bored. Afraid. Impatient. But always *in relationship* to something. *I hate the guy in the White House. I love the guy in the White House. I'm sick of guys being in the White House*…relationships, all.

Consciousness has identities inside of it, such as when you choose to step into a teaching role, or a therapeutic role (say, with clients). And consciousness can drop that identity when it's not needed.

Egoic consciousness can also *be* an identity, like when someone is a fundamentalist form of anything, from a Ku Klux Klan member to a born-again Christian, to a close-minded woke activist. If you're more self-aware, you will know that you have identities that are constructed. If you're less self-aware, you may not know that your identities are constructed, and you may act as if that construct—that temporary identity—is real, permanent, and solid.

At the highest levels, consciousness itself becomes fully self-aware. This means it knows it has an ego, which is part of the whole. Consciousness knows it has personas that sometimes rise up inside of it. It knows that it has psychological shadows, or places that it actually can't see but that can influence thought, feeling, and behavior. In other words, consciousness knows that it has an unconscious part of itself that it can't see. And at its most self-aware, a consciousness can see that everything it *knows* and everything it *is* can only be as big as what it has experienced and what it has known, which isn't that much in the big scale of things.

As I have mentioned, Pink Floyd, in their 1972 album *The Dark Side of the Moon*, said it more eloquently: *all you touch and all you see/is all your life will ever be.* At these very high levels, when something happens in the world that causes a trigger, an emotional reaction, the instinct is to look within rather than to rage outwardly against the perceived problem. Yet even at its most powerful and self-aware, consciousness is still a mind in relationship with *something else.*

Let me give an example from my life, from a men's group I've been part of for many years now. One man in the group was complaining about how his wife can collapse into depression, and how he often felt compelled to manage her, and ended up feeling manipulated by the whole process.

"I know your wife is just that way," another man responded, "and that she spirals down into depression and feels like she just can't do anything in life. And I hate it, because it reminds me of the part of me that wants to lie on the couch and just give up, and I hate that guy inside of myself, so I hate it when I hear you tell stories like this about her. It makes me hate her, but I know I'm just hating that part of myself that I can't stand."

This was someone who was seeing *and catching* his own projected fears in real time so that he could stay in connection to the other man. That is consciousness operating near its highest possible level, deeply self-aware of its own propensity to project and judge others for the things it has and rejects inside of itself. Yet it is still a closed loop: experiencer and experienced, always in a dance of relationship to something else.

At these highest levels, consciousness knows it changes, knows it's self-aware, knows it can be an unreliable recorder of history or subject to having emotion push it to wrong or incomplete conclusions, and knows that it only knows what it knows and nothing else (and that it actually doesn't know all that much). This is why death is so scary to our consciousness, because we can only take solace from death in two ways: magical beliefs (known as religion); or an experience that lets us see through our fear and transmute it, as some do with things like the hallucinogenic South American drink ayahuasca (which, in truth, gives their consciousness a state experience, or a non-ordinary state outside of their egoic view, which is part of what makes it so powerful and can make it quite limited as well).

In my own life experience, I had terrible existential anxiety by my late teens and early twenties because my consciousness could see through itself and know deeply that I was a just a construct, an operating system that was temporary and finite and fallible. I knew I was only as real as the objects in my awareness, and that my consciousness once didn't exist, and in some number of days, week, months, years, or decades, the world as I knew it would cease to exist as well. Scary business. I wanted to know what happened at death and yet found the research frustratingly biased or inherently unsatisfying. What I wanted was proof, and truth where there was none to be had, for even near-death experiences don't tell us what happens when someone fully dies and is unable to return to this world.

To sum up, consciousness includes all of our perceptions, emotions, thoughts, feelings, dreams, beliefs, stories, philosophies, traumas, and life experiences. It includes the full range of our human lives, excluding deep sleep and the deepest spiritual experiences. And it is always *in relationship* to something.

AWARENESS DEFINED

Practitioners of traditional Zen like to say that there are three poisons of the mind, or three ways in which we perpetuate suffering and are unable to see the true nature of our being. These three poisons are attachment, ignorance, and aversion. Here I'd like you to consider *ignorance*, which in the Zen sense means being ignorant of the true nature of your being—essentially *a lack of a proper understanding of the nature of awareness.*

Many people are never actually aware of their awareness, as strange as that might sound. And so, if reading this section doesn't make much sense, it might be because you've never fully experienced the awareness that underlies consciousness, or what some might call *awakened mind*. If you haven't experienced this, or only have fleetingly, know that this book is designed to help you to contact this awareness on your own, but it is my hope that it may be helpful to try and define it first.

Awareness is something else than consciousness, and something that does not change. While consciousness can get very expansive or very contracted, awareness is just aware. It doesn't get big or small, doesn't change in relation to our thoughts of it, isn't impacted when we first contact it, and hasn't evolved or changed since it exists entirely outside of time yet fully within it.

In so many of the experiences I had, my consciousness grew quiet and I instead looked out at the world as awareness itself. I know this place deeply inside of my being, as well as you might know your bedroom, or the look of your partner or child.

When we notice that we have an ego, and that our egos have parts and conditioned behaviors, we become more self-aware. This is our consciousness noticing a part of itself. When we allow an awareness deeper than our consciousness, something that can see the whole of us and all that we can see, we're in touch with something deeper. Some would call this *awake*. Or *aware* of *being aware*.

This kind of awareness notices the changes in consciousness. When we fall into sleep, our consciousness shifts and changes into a dream state, but after some time consciousness ceases to be, and there is only awareness. At some point, consciousness returns with dreaming, and then dreaming gives way to waking up and starting our day. But the awareness is untouched by all of this. Dream yoga, it should be noted, can teach us to remain self-aware as consciousness shifts from waking to dreaming, and we can dream lucidly—consciously knowing that we are dreaming. This is fairly straightforward, and most people can succeed in having some kinds of lucid dreams without too much practice. But there's a deeper skill, which is remaining aware as consciousness fades and there is only awareness left, in deep sleep, and then watching the dreamer come back into existence, and then watching "you" come back into existence.

Awareness, when we contact it with our consciousness, is always *here* (never "there"). Always present. It can see but not be seen. Awareness is the ultimate subjectivity, only ever looking out at the world but unknowable to itself because there is nothing to know about it. It's here at our birth and it's here at our death, and it remains constant throughout our lives.

In the quiet of meditation, we can reside inside of *this* awareness (not *our* awareness, for we do not have *it*.) If you believe you "have" awareness, this really means your ego believes you've captured enlightenment, something that is quite impossible.

All egos are, by their nature, dualistic—it is how the ego operates. So when an ego believes it is enlightened, spiritual narcissism is always the result. Remember that you cannot keep your spiritual insight for yourself, because *you* reside inside of *it*, not the other way around. And so, from this realization you can watch your consciousness arise. Your ego arises, even as that ego is trying to keep what it finds for itself. The paradox is you can allow the dance of life to flow through you, as you, which can transform your ego so long as you don't try and keep what you find for yourself.

WHAT IS SPIRITUAL, ANYWAY?

Awareness can't be changed, can't be moved, has never spoken, and although it's not static, it's not dynamic either. You can see *as* awareness, but you can't see *it* as an object of your consciousness, which is what far too many meditators try and do. You can allow your conscious attention to be on something like the breath, and in so doing, sometimes, the awareness that is always arising suddenly *is all that you are*. Then, as awareness itself, your little ego, with all your dramas, opinions, stories, contractions, traumas, identities, neuroses, and attachments, is seen as simply arising within this ever-present, ever-unchanging awareness-that-is-really-you. This is the thing that was here before the Big Bang, and will be here after the Big Crunch, that which came before you came into existence, and that will be here after your ego goes out of existence, an awareness not bound by time or physics or space or mathematics or logic.

As mentioned in the last chapter, many of us have an experience of this awareness at some point in our lives, but then after it *seems* to fade, we try and claim the experience of ourselves. When we speak about "ignorance" in Zen, this is where we are pointing—where language creates the very problem that can prevent genuine insight because people are practicing with the wrong idea—*ignorance*—of what awakening really is.

Awareness exists in relationship to nothing because it includes everything in the manifest and unmanifest world. Awareness isn't located in your belly or your third eye or your heart, which is why we sometimes say it is empty, because it has no locus, no central location. Consciousness seems to exist in the head, more or less, and as we evolve we can also experience our consciousness in our body as well. But awareness doesn't exist anywhere. We also say awareness is empty because awareness is just aware, nothing more. There are no stories here, no karmas, no identities, no morality, no good or evil, no nothing. But also something.

Now, for some readers this might be a bit like an itch you can't quite reach, something irritatingly close and far away at the same time. Other readers may have experienced this for themselves, and yet their consciousness seems to override their awareness, so that the latter becomes nothing but a memory.

This is another problem with our spiritual identity, because thinking we've lost something that we are (awareness itself) sends us looking for something that we already have and are. In the words of the seventeenth century Zen Master Hakiun:

> *Sentient beings are from the very beginning Buddhas.*
> *It is like ice and water; apart from water, no ice can exist.*
> *Outside sentient beings, where do we find the Buddhas?*
>
> *Not knowing how near the Truth is, we seek it far away.*
> *What a pity! We are like a person who, in the midst of water,*
> *cries in thirst so imploringly. We are like the child of a rich house*
> *who has wandered away among the poor.* —From The Song of Zazen,
> *as translated by Mondo Zen and Junpo Roshi*

The intersection between these two things—consciousness and awareness—was the tidal pool in which I was caught; I had no way of knowing that I was moving back and forth between these two perspectives, and no way to understand how to find stability and insight from what was happening, instead of the increasing uncertainty, chaos, and suffering in utter silence. Some of my experiences were of a spiritual or illuminated ego consciousness, where my relationship to other things felt divine in its origin. But other times I simply was awareness itself, looking out on and as the manifest universe.

THE WAY OUT IS THROUGH

In the mid-1990s I moved from New York City to Philadelphia, where it was cheaper and easier to live. I worked as a short-order cook for $5 an hour, working full time from 5 p.m. to 1 a.m. five days a week—all for a $200 weekly salary. I wrote a lot, trying to finish my first novel, and tried to manage what was happening to me.

WHAT IS SPIRITUAL, ANYWAY?

Increasingly desperate, I finally sought out a psychologist, an intern since I couldn't afford to pay a practicing psychologist, who asked me not once but twice if I heard voices.

"I already told you no," I said the second time. "Twice." It seemed she thought I was crazy, too.

One of my dearest friends at the time, who is one of my dearest friends still, insisted I read Ken Wilber's *Sex, Ecology, Spirituality*,[10] and finally I relented. Sitting on a dirty cutting board in the cramped and hot kitchen of the Dawson Street Pub in Philly, I read the book with an increasing sense of awe and burst into tears at one point, realizing that what I was experiencing had some kind of explanation aside from "crazy." Wilber put my many experiences into a context of spiritual unfolding—something I had no idea existed. He introduced me to some of the great mystics I had never heard of, and to their own words, which so mirrored what was happening to me. For the first time in a decade I felt not dread but excitement, and was able to view these "trans-personal" experiences I was having inside of a model that not only said I wasn't going crazy but that I was actually on an extraordinary path!

Next, I found a Buddhist psychotherapist, no small feat in Philly in the mid-1990s. He was unfazed by my strange experiences and was able to hold them as quite separate from other issues affecting me. He also was familiar with Wilber's work and knew enough about spiritual unfolding to give me his own book recommendations so that I could better understand what was happening.

I braved the "spiritual" and "new age" sections of bookstores, where I had to stomach books on angels, Atlantis, psychics, chakras, and weird-looking men like Adi Da and Rajneesh peering off their book covers with creepy, faraway eyes. But I did find some needle-in-the-haystack authors who wrote seriously

---

10 *Sex, Ecology, and Spirituality* (Ken Wilber, Sex, Ecology, Spirituality: The Spirit of Evolution [Boulder, CO: Shambhala Publications, 1995]) is an epic masterwork by Ken Wilber, well over 800 pages long, that provides a comprehensive look at Eastern mysticism and Western psychological development, among other weighty topics. The book attempts to bring mysticism and psychology together, and to provide a map of the evolution of consciousness that could include both Freud and Buddha. Wilber would also introduce his 4 Quadrant model of reality here. In later books, Wilber would abandon his model of development outlined in this book for one that is more nuanced and more fully explained in his book, *Integral Spirituality*. (Shambhala Publications, 2007)

and skillfully about non-ordinary states of consciousness using the tools of science and of rationality, the only tools I was willing to trust at the time. In addition to Wilber, these included writers like Stan and Christina Groff, best-selling author Michael Crichton (his book *Travels* chronicles his own extensive and eye-opening experiences of non-ordinary states of consciousness), Michael Murphy (*The Future of the Body*), and Daniel P. Brown, among others.

I learned that while many of the experiences I was having were ones that some people spent years or even decades trying to have for themselves, a great number of people had been like me and had these kinds of things materialize suddenly and seemingly without warning. It seemed that alcoholism, depression, and anxiety were common side effects, as were disrupted careers and marriages. Fortunately for me, I had no career to lose, I worked in a bar where alcohol abuse was the norm, and anxiety was such a part of my personality that I hardly even noticed it. My girlfriend and I were inseparable, even though she too knew nothing of the experiences I was having because it would take another fifteen years for me to learn to trust others with my suffering.

By my mid-twenties I had begun to meditate, and in 1998 found myself at the Philadelphia Shambhala Center to hear a woman with the mystical-sounding name of Lama Tsering Everest. She was one of the senior students of a Tibetan teacher named Chagdud Tulka Rinpoche, who was then head of one of the four schools of Tibetan Buddhism (the Nyingma School). She would become my first meditation teacher and led the way for me to enter Buddhism formally in the Vajrayana tradition, by taking vows under her not long before my thirtieth birthday.

It seemed I was now on *a path* instead of stumbling in circles by myself. I was getting guidance from people who studied mindfulness formally and who had spent much of their lives training their minds in very specific ways. And my world was starting to change.

THE PURPOSE OF PRACTICE

A reasonable reader might ask: Why did I start a practice? After all, I was having all of these spiritual experiences without effort. That is true. However, the more experiences I had and the deeper they were, the more painful it was

WHAT IS SPIRITUAL, ANYWAY?

to live inside of my limited and limiting ego view. I'd had dozens and dozens of profound experiences, but they came and went just like any other experience. While they did leave a part of themselves behind, none were strong enough or deep enough to fundamentally transform who I was.

At thirty I was still a painfully shy and awkward man, largely crippled by anxiety and uncertainty, unsure of my professional path, and with a self-worth that hovered just above worthless. I was mostly a passenger in my own life, very unhappy in my relationship of over ten years (through no fault of my then-partner), and in my work, and I felt largely trapped and victimized by life. All of those spiritual experiences had translated into little lived transformation.

For most people, a spiritual practice is about finding a better mood, a little more emotional equinity, a touch of wisdom, a sense of deeper harmony with nature and her rhythms, or maybe even a community of like-minded people to spend Sundays with. These are perfectly valid reasons to take up a spiritual practice, and they will reap the practitioner some rewards, without a doubt.

But they will not liberate you.

I wanted liberation because I'd touched liberation with my own two hands, and nothing short of it would do.

Junpo loved to tell this story about Chögyam Trungpa Rinpoche,[11] who he met back in the 1970s. Junpo and some friends went to see Trungpa speak. Trungpa had a reputation for being very late to his talks, so they showed up for an 8 p.m. talk at 10 p.m., only to find Trungpa had still not made an appearance.

---

11 Chögyam Trungpa Rinpoche was a controversial Tibetan spiritual teacher who largely set aside his traditional training to teach his Western students in a novel and highly unconventional way. He was very fond of alcohol and drugs, as well as sex with his students. He was a proponent of what came to be known as *crazy wisdom*, something my teacher Junpo powerfully rejected (that story can be found in my book of Junpo's life, *A Heart Blown Open*).

Junpo and his friends chatted, passing the time, and at around 10:30, Trungpa came out from behind a screen, wearing his usual three-piece suit and heavy glasses, a goblet of sake in his hand. He was visibly intoxicated and looked over the crowd while swaying a little.

Everyone grew quiet. Trungpa was becoming quite famous, had numerous well-selling and influential books in print, and had co-founded Naropa University in Boulder, Colorado. He surveyed the crowd, took a big swallow from his goblet, and stepped up to the mic. "Go home," he said, smiling. "There's still time."

And with that, he walked off the stage. Five words were the entirety of his talk. The crowd was stunned into silence and, after they realized he was gone, rumbled with disapproval. Confused conversations broke out. When Junpo realized Trungpa wasn't coming back he roared with laughter.

Junpo told the story to me exactly as I told it here. And he told me this story many, many times. The truth was I didn't get it, at all. I had no idea why Junpo laughed, or why he kept telling me this same story. I admit I pretended to laugh as if I knew, but truthfully, I didn't know what the hell Trungpa meant or why Junpo loved it so much. It sounded like drunken buffoonery to me.

Many years later I was on a Zen retreat and feeling the pain and the tension between the state of awareness I could sometimes access and the state of consciousness where I spent most of my life. The difference between them had become extraordinarily painful to me, and I thought of Junpo's story.

Go home. There's still time.

And it hit me: Once you get a taste of awakening, once you see past yourself for the first time—*really* see past yourself—*there is no going back.* You can try and fit the new you back into your old life, but awareness and liberation will call to you endlessly, and eventually you will have no choice but to surrender yourself onto the path of awakening, or to live knowing that you're only seeing a tiny sliver of what's really happening in your world. Either choice has serious repercussions for one's life. Some of us get off of the spiritual path for good reasons: career, kids, a desire to sink our teeth into life instead of spending hours and hours on a meditation cushion, but it's impossible to forget the call once you've known it in your being.

Go home. There's still time.

When I was attending dozens of weeklong Zen retreats in my thirties, it was not lost on me that it was very rare for a retreatant to be in their forties. Almost all of us were either younger than forty or over fifty, something that had perplexed me until I realized that for most of us, our forties are about establishing ourselves, and the intensive deconstructive container of a Zen retreat is simply not conducive to that. Only after fifty, when mortality's whispers grow louder with stiffening backs and increasing grays do people return to find a deeper truth than their egos.

And so Trungpa was warning that room of people: Go home. There's still time to pretend you're not the Buddha, to live your days ignorant of the truth of who and what you really are. I might extend that same warning to you, dear reader. Put this book down. There's still time!

IS IT AS SIMPLE AS "YOU ARE WHAT YOU SEEK?"

I was in my mid-thirties at this point. Sometimes I would be in an egoless and nondual state for months at a time. I believed at some point these states would become permanent, and I would no longer have to work on my spiritual practice. I thought the depth of my spiritual insight would transform my ego, and that would be that.

After all, I said pretty much as much in the previous chapter of this book—you are what you seek, and all you need to do is allow it, right? Yes, that's true. That is undeniably true from my perspective. And it's also not that simple, for I had things a bit backward in two different ways.

First, I was under the belief, *the very strong belief*, that enlightenment was something that happened *to* you and that once it happened *to* you, that was it. After all, awakening experiences came to me with the frequency of the full moon, and I didn't do much to create those events. I believed that eventually those experiences would simply silence my ego and I would be off the wheel of life, off the wheel of suffering. I would no longer struggle against anything. I would no longer have bad or good days. I wouldn't fear death, or life, or anything. I would simply *be*, and there would no longer be any need to do something like practice. Waking up was like getting a degree: Once it was done, it was done, and all one had to do was sit back and enjoy the view. Enlightenment, in other words, had a finish line, so in my conversations I would say things such as, "After awakening...."

This idea was fueled by the fact my own spiritual insights had largely come outside of any practice, proving that sort of work wasn't necessary in order to have those kinds of insights. And I'd lived inside of this truth of being beyond ego, sometimes for months at a time.

For instance, after one especially deep insight on retreat, I came home to my then girlfriend. At the time, we had been deeply involved in the TV show *Mad Men*, but once home I had no interest in it whatsoever. I had no interest in reading, or doing anything except sitting and looking at a wall. I did my work to make money. She and I made love. I was fully present to her and my life, but there was just no noise in my world. I didn't need to get away from anything and lived fully inside of the moment. TV and books no longer held any interest to me.

Needless to say, my girlfriend was a little freaked out, but when this state of being began to fade, the pain was almost unbearable. As I became "trapped" again inside of my Keith-ness, in tears I called a mentor, Doshin M.J. Nelson Roshi (then merely a Zen priest) to help provide some understanding of what was happening to me. He helped me see the trouble was my ego, which was still badly fractured from unresolved wounding and childhood trauma, which is to say that what I was lacking was integration. I was like Eckhart Tolle sitting on his park benches for two years, cut off from his humanity and cut off from human contact. That was how I had been living and, while it was painful to be back inside of my ego, that was largely because my ego was largely a painful place to be. Like Junpo, I would need to do many hundreds of hours of therapy to get underneath of the deep wounding that had shaped so much of me.

Put more simply: I had liberated myself *from* the world, but true awakening means being liberated *in* the world. And to do that, I needed to integrate the mess of my egoic being. So do you.

WHAT IS SPIRITUAL, ANYWAY?

The second problem was that most teachers had been saying the same thing for more than 1,000 years, a thing that today's nondual teachers like Eckhart Tolle and Adyashanti repeat: *The grand ultimate truth, enlightenment, is by definition fully here now.* The grand ultimate truth cannot come and go; the only thing that can come and go is our ability to realize it. Makes sense, yes? The deepest, timeless truth of the universe is not bound by us or our perceptions of it any more than a sunset goes away because we stop looking at it.

And to be clear: This is a vital truth you *must* realize inside of your practice. Otherwise, you are chasing something you already own, trying to "discover" or "find" enlightenment, which is like trying to "discover" or "find" your own face. *How* you do this is the question, and different teachers have different solutions.

It is true that you have what you seek. That is absolutely true. And it is true that you must get out of the way to realize what you already have. You can't seek what you already have, and are. You can only realize it by allowing it to be. This also is completely and totally true.

But the truth is also that most of us cannot keep our egos out of the way quite enough to allow awakening to be fully experienced, and therefore to fully transform, our minds. And it is not so easy as simply awakening, because there is no such thing as "after" awakening. That very idea is a prison that confuses even the most skilled and devoted practitioner. There is no "after enlightenment" because there's nothing after this moment. Being fully integrated means that there is no separation between your ordinary mind and the awareness that allows it to arise. Both unfold in a perfect dance of an absolute view and a relative one, moving out from this moment.

The easiest way I've come to understand this reality is that if I'm having experiences, then I am in relationship to them. That is, by definition, consciousness, or *ego view*. It might be an incredibly lovely ego view. I may have divine premonitions, a rich life of inner prayer, be in communion with departed souls or ancestors, dialog with the Creator, and many other powerful things that spiritual people do and that I myself have done. But all of those things are in relationship *to* something else.

When I move past having an experience, which by definition arises in time and ends in time, there is a part of me that is always present for every experience. This part of me doesn't come and go; it is present for my deepest spiritual experience and my most human (and petty) one. This witnessing capacity, this *awareness* that lies underneath our consciousness, is where I had yet to take my seat. From a place of this "eye of the spirit," as Ken Wilber might say, I am able to watch the unfolding of the world and of myself with utter clarity *and with deep feeling*. There is as much magic, *even more magic*, in the chirp of a bird as there is in a thousand mystical experiences. This is another reason why in Zen we say "ordinary mind is the way," because from awareness the comings and goings of the ordinary mind are as spectacular as the most sacred experience of the divine.

Liberation comes not from freeing ourselves of this world but rather integrating ourselves fully into it, turning away from nothing and embracing all that we encounter here. The rest of this book will explore how, exactly, we can do that.

CHAPTER 3

The Dignity and the Disaster of Our Egos

Liberation comes from being free *within* life, not from it. This requires that you find a more sophisticated understanding of what your ego is and is not, because there is no liberation without bringing your ego along for the ride. That is one of the most common misunderstandings people have of spiritual awakening—that somehow you simply transcend your ego altogether. This is absolutely not the case. Your relationship to your ego will be transformed, but your ego will remain much as it is, for better or for worse.

As I mentioned before, in traditional Zen there are three poisons of the mind, or three ways that we perpetuate suffering and are unable to see the true nature of our being. These three poisons are attachment, ignorance, and aversion. Here I invite you to explore *attachment*.

The ego is defined by its thinking and, on the whole, we tend to believe what we think. And that makes sense. Lots of our thoughts are, to state the obvious, helpful. This includes everything from what we're thinking of having for dinner to how to dress when the weather turns cold. Science, philosophy, engineering, good parenting, paying your taxes, and a thousand other things all rely on using our thoughts as tools to achieve something that helps us to live life more fully. Our opinions on the environment, racial justice, our nation's history, the political party in power, our favorite sports team, and our last relationship (or our current one)—all arise from thinking. We tend to believe our own notions because we don't do a very good job of discerning our functional thoughts ("I want salmon for dinner") with those that are judgmental ("People who eat fish are wrong because they're destroying the environment"). When we dig a little deeper into those charged thoughts—our opinions, our deeply-held beliefs, our views of what's right and wrong with the world—it's not hard to find an embarrassing number of times when we were terribly confused in our thinking and were, in fact, wrong.

What makes this a humbling affair for those of us paying attention is that being clear in our thinking is no guarantee that we're correct. How many times have you felt righteous indignation over a perceived wrong but, days, weeks, or years later understand a more nuanced truth than you could see at the time? We can look at extreme examples to see how far clear but deluded thinking can go: Stalin, Pol Pot, Mao, and Hitler were all very clear in their thinking and all came to horribly wrong conclusions about the world, and a hundred million or more died as a result. Our clarity of thought and our conviction about the rightness of our thoughts are no guarantees of us being correct, or moral, or just. For me personally, when I feel really right about something—be it in politics, intimate relationships, or culture—I now know to slow way down and to look harder for what I might be missing, because I always find something.

Putting this another way is bringing back what I said in the "About This Book?" section. Much of what we think is real to us, but it's not true. It might be real that you think Democrats are in the business of eating children and worshipping Satan, but it's not true. You might think it's real that the earth is flat and the round earth is a grand conspiracy, but it's not true. It might seem real that your upbringing has vastly limited your potential, but that's also not true. So much of what we perceive as being real is not, in fact, true. We discover that once we dig underneath and look more carefully at how we're constraining reality with our ideas of what *is* and *isn't* real. We'll dig more into what is true later in the book.

Part of the confusion of believing our thoughts comes from the powerful illusion that our ego is a solid and permanent self, and that our consciousness is a set and concrete thing that looks out at the world in a stable and steady manner, not changing from day to day or from year to year or from decade to decade—or at least not changing very much. We often hear others say, "People don't change," and that seems true on a gut level. We think this is true because we tell ourselves a story about ourselves—that our sense of self is a solid and stable thing. Let's take a moment to slow down here and see if this is a story that holds up to scrutiny.

WHY WE FIGHT WARS

Junpo used to say that our egos are a *process* and not a *self*. Which at first might not sound like that profound a statement, unless you take it literally. What if you, right now, as you read this sentence, were actually a *process* and not a self? A process is malleable, for one. It's a combination of many things that, taken together, create something new. You can make cars with a certain kind of process or write code for your operating system. You can have a process that educates your children (a Montessori school uses a very different process to educate children than a public one), a process for organizing your closets, and one for how to properly train the dog. But what if *you* were a process as well? A process is fluid, malleable, impermanent, and open to change based on new inputs. A self is fixed, boundaried, feels permanent, and is, generally speaking, closed to any significant change. What if you decided to look at yourself as a process instead of a self?

As human beings, we create our sense of self through the stories told to us, that we tell ourselves, and that we tell others. We believe these stories, sometimes with a literal religious fervor. When they are our personal stories, they make up our identities—where we were born, what our childhoods were like, what happened to us and didn't happen to us, what we once thought and what we now know. When they are our collective stories, they make up our worldview—a master race, a privileged group, a marginalized people, a newly-empowered gender.

In places like the United States, new views are emerging telling the American story from perspectives of race, inequality, power, and gender. These stories are different from the older ones and more inclusive of multiple historical perspectives (or at least that's the goal). Our personal story might be one of being very religious, or the story of being a rational scientist, or the story of being a caring antiracist, among many possible ones. In both cases, the personal and the collective, we are saying certain things are true about us and our world, and other things are not true.

Yet if we step back we might notice something hidden right below the surface. Some people see the world through the story of their religion, their "one and true" faith. They often demand we believe their story, or else. Others look at the very same world and see it composed of rationality, science, and the scientific method. In this mode of perception, data, not belief, form the backbone of a truth that is grounded in an ever-evolving worldview and is ever-evolving. Others still look at this world and see it full of "isms"—sexism, racism, ableism, and nationalism among other things, all based in privilege with victims and oppressors and rescuers in a constant swirl. They see everything, including science and rationality (and certainly religion) inside of a grand narrative of power. All three of these ways of seeing the world think the other two are just simply *wrong*, and quite possibly evil to boot.

"If we can just get rid of those other two worldviews," the religious man says, "the world would be ordered and Godly."

"If we can just get rid of those other two worldviews," the scientific woman says, "the world would be rational and fair."

"If we can just get rid of those other two worldviews," the university scholar says, "the world would be just and equitable."

All three of these views can't be true *at the same time*. Yet all might have a piece of the truth, an important part of the whole in which we all find ourselves. From a Zen perspective, we would say the world is big enough for a conservative Christian, a scientist, and a university scholar. And we could say that all three have important things to say about the nature of our world. Some of their views can be helpful to us as we live our lives. There is no problem with these views in and of themselves. The problem is with their, and our, attachment to those views. Wars are fought not over clashing ideologies, but over attachment to clashing ideologies.

If we allow that Junpo may have been correct in that *we are a process and not a self*, this makes for a much more interesting relationship to the stories we tell ourselves about ourselves, and about our world. A *process* isn't something that gets red in the face arguing about politics, but a self *is*. Does the world need more selves, convinced they are correct, shouting into the web about how right they are, and how evil, stupid, or complicit everyone else is? Do you find peace and harmony in being *right about things?* As you look back at the whole of your life, are your happiest moments the ones when you were proven right? Somehow, I very much doubt that is the case. So what do you really want?

THE FALLIBLE YOU

For some of us the idea that our ego is a process and not a self might be totally obvious. For those who are still not so sure, let's take a deeper look at this seemingly solid sense we have of ourselves.

As we covered in the last chapter, when we're identified solely with our consciousness, it can radically shape how we perceive reality. On the mild side, a bad mood might make us experience our world as unfriendly and hostile, while a good mood has us experience all the positive things around us. Every day, pleasant and unpleasant things happen; we often filter which one is "real" based on our moods. On the more extreme side, our consciousness can have us seeing all kinds of evil or conspiracies in the world where *they don't exist*.

Those with mental illness can live in hell realms that are generated largely by the distortions of their minds. In the wonderful novel (and great movie adaptation) *The Life of Pi*, the narrator, Pi Patel, turns out to be unreliable: We can't trust him to show us what's really happening versus what's happening in his imagination. This literary device, the unreliable narrator, has been used in countless novels, from Holden Caulfield in *The Catcher in the Rye* to Humbert Humbert in *Lolita*. And yet how reliable a narrator would we be of our own lives? At a minimum, we can agree that our consciousness can be an unreliable way to gauge what's real and what's not, even if just in the simple ways described at the start of this paragraph.

While our egos feel stable, with just casual reflection we can see that our beliefs and ideas and sense of self have evolved and changed over the course of our lifetimes, so much so that we might not even like our younger selves if we were able to sit down and talk with them. We certainly might find some of their opinions a bit hard to stomach. We don't notice the changes to ourselves because they're so gradual, but anyone who's been to a twenty-fifth high school reunion will walk away knowing that most everyone there is quite unlike their high school selves (thank goodness). And our sense of self can change with intoxicants like alcohol or pot, become unconscious in dreaming, and vanish entirely in deep sleep only to reemerge as we awaken. LSD, DMT, ayahuasca, ketamine, and other powerful drugs can radically alter or even dissolve the sense of self entirely, yet leave something behind that is able to witness what's happening. Changes to the brain, like dementia, strokes, or Parkinson's disease can alter how the self is constructed and how others perceive it.

The Harvard psychologist Dan Gilbert's book, *Stumbling on Happiness*, illustrates that humans don't notice just how radically they change over just a ten-year span. The change happens outside of our awareness, and Gilbert asks the question: Why does our present self so often make decisions that our future selves will regret—the ill-conceived tattoo, the dead-end relationship, the putting clothes we don't need on a credit card with a 27 percent compounding interest rate?

> *What I want to convince you is that all of us are walking around with an illusion, an illusion that history, our personal history, has just come to an end, that we have just recently become the people that we were always meant to be—and will be for the rest of our lives…*
>
> *Time is a powerful force. It transforms our preferences. It reshapes our values. It alters our personalities. We seem to appreciate this fact, **but***

only in retrospect. Only when we look backwards do we realize how much change happens in a decade. It's as if, for most of us, the present is a magic time. It's a watershed on the timeline. It's the moment at which we finally become ourselves. **Human beings are works in progress that mistakenly think they're finished.** The person you are right now is as transient, as fleeting and as temporary as all the people you've ever been.[12]

Despite this, we cling to this idea that we have a solid and stable self, rather than a solid and stable *process* that generates a self over time, and *the self that gets generated changes.*

Let me explain: You think, right now, you're more or less the same self you were a decade ago, but you're not. That self has changed in many ways—maybe you've become more expansive in your views, more self-aware, more conscious, and more loving. Or maybe you've become more neurotic, more addicted, more closed off, more certain of just how fucking right you are, and more likely to wage war against those unlike you. But this self that you think is you, generated as a process, is fluid and changing, not static and solid. You, in other words, are as ethereal as a summer storm—here one moment and gone the next. The process that generates the storm lives on to generate other storms, just as the process that generates you goes on to generate other versions of you.

Because that is far closer to the truth. Despite this, we insist on holding our personas as if they're solid things: *spiritual, straight, patriot, queer, artist, teacher, loser, fat, unlovable, broken, empowered, divine.* Those identities can be helpful or harmful, but all of them are transient, impermanent, constructed, and a tepid reflection of the undefinable mysterious process that each human being actually is. Our stories of ourselves are just a collection of thoughts over time. And we're not our thoughts. So how can we be the stories we tell of ourselves?

---

12 https://www.ted.com/talks/dan_gilbert_the_psychology_of_your_future_self/transcript?language=en#t-125989

Let's take one more example. There is overwhelming data that we remember our own lives poorly, but we *think* we remember them with crystal clarity.[13] Professor Elizabeth Loftus has made a career of proving that we are actually terrible at remembering things and that it's quite easy to implant false memories we will be convinced are real. Her research helped to undermine the power of the eyewitness testimony, which for decades was assumed to be the nearly unassailable gold standard in American courts—until she proved how fallible memory actually is.

The Innocence Project, which uses DNA testing to exonerate those wrongfully convicted of crimes, has reported that 73 percent of the 239 convictions overturned through DNA testing were based on eyewitness testimony. That means that three out of four eyewitnesses in these cases, swearing under oath and undoubtedly convinced they were being truthful, were just plain wrong![14]

In addition to having terrible memories, we are also highly prone to biases in how we view and assess information, due to cognitive bias (phenomena such as the Dunning-Kruger effect) and implicit bias (based on attitudes and stereotypes). And when it comes to making critical and big decisions, most of us make them more for unconscious emotional reasons than for logical and rational ones.[15]

The reason for this is that we're a process and not a self, and a process is always in process—never stable, never static, highly mutable, changeable, malleable, prone to being influenced, often wrong, and always partial. Yet we insist there's a solid "me" driving the bus, despite all the evidence to the contrary, and we believe our thoughts even when we're presented with overwhelming evidence that they cannot be trusted, and we cannot possibly be

---

13 Elizabeth Loftus and Katherine Ketcham, *Witness for the Defense: The Accused, the Eyewitness and the Expert Who Puts Memory on Trial* (New York: St. Martin's Griffin, 1992).
14 Hal Arkowitz and Scott O. Lilienfeld, "Why Science Tells Us Not to Rely on Eyewitness Accounts," Scientific American online, January 1, 2010, https://www.scientificamerican.com/article/do-the-eyes-have-it.
15 Paul Thagard and Allison Barnes, "Emotional Decisions," in *Proceedings of the Eighteenth Annual Conference of the Cognitive Science Society* (Mahwah NJ: Erlbaum, 2996): 426-429.

just our thoughts. The stubborn story of "self" fights to maintain itself against all evidence to the contrary, even stories of us being very spiritual people.

My first spiritual teacher, Lama Tsering Everest, once said to me, "Keith, the Buddha told us that the world is suffering, that suffering has a cause, and that the cause is I. Remove the I, and you will remove the suffering."

Letting go of our attachment to this fallible idea of self allows us to experience the world as it really is instead of how we want to believe it is. This is a powerful insight and a critical step toward the humility that underlies all true wisdom.

THE CONDITIONED US

Well into middle age, Junpo began to confront the demons of his childhood and how powerfully they had defined so much of his life, from his struggles with narcissism, to his problematic relationships with women, to his at times heroic use of LSD. Half a decade after his realization of an ego being a process and not a self, after six hours in deep meditation, he came to a second, equally profound realization: that *process is entirely conditioned.* The process of self, he went on to realize, is conditioned biologically, culturally, and psychologically, and that conditioning is *very strong and nearly absolute for most of us.*

Most people I know balk at this statement when they hear it. After all, it seems self-evident that I choose my girlfriend, my diet, the car I drive, the music I listen to, the friends I have, the sports I watch, and on and on. As I sit here and type into my computer, it seems reasonable for me to conclude that I am a totally (or at least almost totally) free being a man who makes all of the major and even minor decisions in his life from a place of choice. And it does seem reasonable, because I can choose to stop typing and get a sip of water at any point as an act of sheer will and freedom.

Yet I'd like to, once more, slow this down and take a deeper look underneath what might really be happening.

Consider an avatar, a made-up human we'll call John, who is a typical American male of thirty-six years of age. John works hard, plays hard, and isn't especially introspective, just like many of us.

John knows that he chooses his girlfriend. After all, what other truth could there be? Yet maybe John also starts to learn that he has a history of choosing women who have an avoidant attachment style, meaning their default setting is to always be "looking for the exits" in their relationships. Avoidantly-attached humans (like the one writing this book) can struggle with intimacy because their default setting is self-preservation via independence, something learned in their childhoods. Parents can create avoidant tendencies by being too absent or too badly attuned to the emotional needs of their child. But either way, the child is forced to care for their own emotional needs, and this gets coded into how they understand relationships.[16]

Maybe John also begins to see that he chooses women who have a hard time trusting men, and who also are secretive about their inner worlds. And maybe John would have never seen this pattern, except a friend points it out to him. He might find out, if he were to do some work with a guide like a therapist or psychologist, that his relationship to his mother might have left wounding that greatly impacted who he chooses to date. John's "free" choices around his dating life might actually be far more constrained by the very strong preferences of his unconscious mind.

John believes he and he alone chooses the car he drives, his diet, his music, and everything else. Yet with each of these choices, we can see where John is conditioned by his culture. If he's an American, he's not driving a rickshaw or taking a *tuk tuk* to work. If he's "a man's man," that probably means he drives a Camaro or a Ram truck and not a powder-blue Prius. John's testosterone is high, which translates into him watching a lot of porn in his downtime, and in getting into some fistfights when he was a younger man. He watches American football because, well, he's an American and finds European football incredibly boring. He loves rock and roll because that's what his older brother listened to. He eats what nutritionists call the "standard American diet" of processed foods, sugary drinks, and

---

16 The science of attachment is fascinating and this is just a simplistic overview. Interested readers should read *Attached: The New Science of Adult Attachment and How It Can Help You Find—and Keep—Love* by Amir Levine and Rachel S. F. Heller (TarcherPerigee, 2010).

generous portions of alcohol because that's what's cheap and easy and tastes good to him.

John might very well smack you in the face if you suggested any of those choices were anything but completely and totally his, born of his own free will. And yet with a simple, cursory, and not particularly deep analysis, we can see that most of these choices that seem free are really conditioned by biology, psychology, or culture. The freedom John thinks he has is, at best, partial, and at worst a total illusion.

We are all Johns. Some of us realize this conditioning and some of us do not, but the data is simply overwhelming. In the realm of phycology, our early years have been proven to massively influence how we behave in relationships and the ways we respond to pressures we experience therein. Maybe you love too easily, or don't let people very far in. Maybe you don't trust others too easily. Maybe you're guarded in love, wary of someone getting too close to your heart. Maybe you give care away with ease and joy. Maybe you think that only true love can really save you, or that love is mostly just a trick of the brain. All of these ideas are rooted in how you experienced love as a child.[17] Yet we hilariously think we choose our love in some kind of objective manner.

We know that we are programmed culturally, which is why we are told about things like the patriarchy, and that society should not be able to tell women what they can and cannot be (which is really just programming them in a better way, but still programming them). Cultural conditioning means that heterosexual men in India can, and do, hold hands, but in Texas they do not. Racial justice theories are predicated on the fact and the evidence that we are all enculturated with unconscious presumptions around race and gender. Our culture largely dictates how we view drug use, the role of individuality, and human sexuality, to name three among hundreds of cultural variants.[18]

---

[17] Bessel van der Kolk, *The Body Keeps the Score: Brain, Mind, and Body in the Transformation of Trauma* (London: Penguin Books, 2015).
[18] Elliot Aronson, *The Social Animal*, 12th ed. (New York: Worth Publishers, 2018).

Our biological conditioning is obvious. All humans are born and will die. Three copies of chromosome 21 will cause Down syndrome, while a certain defect in chromosome 4 will cause the fatally degenerative Huntington's disease 100 percent of the time (that's what killed one of my closest friends at the age of forty-two in an inarguable demonstration of biological determinacy).

Mutations in BRCA1 or BRCA2 genes significantly increase your risk of certain kinds of cancer. Biological females give birth and can generate milk for their offspring. The top 50 fighters in the world are all biologically male because at the extreme end of the bell curve of aggression, you'll only find biological men. However, in the middle of that bell curve, where the vast majority of us live, you'll find plenty of biological women who can whoop the asses of plenty of biological men. And as the trans-rights movement has pointed out, altering biology with hormones and surgery can have profound impacts on how one experiences their own sex and gender[19] and how society experiences them, thereby proving the point: we are biologically conditioned. (In the next chapter, we'll take a closer look into how our brain's organization is impacted by both evolution and childhood experiences, and what that means for our conditioning and for our capacity to choose enlightenment.)

We can know that we're conditioned biologically, culturally, and psychologically, but that knowledge alone doesn't give us any freedom from that conditioning. For instance, no amount of willpower can change the conditioning from our childhood—it's there and it shapes many of the choices we make, like it or not. How we feel about that fact doesn't change the fact one bit, nor does knowing how that trait came to be. For instance, if I had a mother who was badly attuned to my emotions as a child, and I'm highly avoidantly attached as an adult, knowing this and knowing the connection between the two will do very little to impact my behavior, which is happening almost entirely through my unconscious decision making. Likewise, if I don't want to be enculturated as an American but refuse to leave the country, it's

---

19 If we hold that sex is biological and binary and gender is cultural and fluid.

very hard to change that cultural conditioning. And, of course, wishing I was a woman without doing anything to change either my appearance or my biology will make it very hard to get the new reality I want reflected back to me, or even to come forth from within me.

The good news from an egoic position is that awareness of the fact that we are almost entirely conditioned is a critical first step to being able to see our conditioning for what it is, and to put our attention in the places where we can wiggle a pinky into our conditioning and begin to recondition ourselves to be freer and have more choice. We can indeed *influence* our conditioning, with work.

Your attachment style, for instance: If it's avoidant, anxious, or disorganized, you can slowly change it to be secure, but that usually takes years of concerted effort with a talented therapist or psychologist. You can influence your biological conditioning by taking testosterone or estrogen, hitting the gym hard, eating high-quality food, getting enough rest, and taking targeted supplements. And you can influence your cultural conditioning by becoming as aware as you can of the ways in which your culture has programmed you to think about certain things, from sports to gender to race. The conditioning remains, but we can gain some awareness around it, which can allow for the choice that will make up much of the remainder of this book.

IS EGO AN ENEMY ON THE PATH?

We have established the ego is a conditioned entity. Being "egotistical" implies that too much ego makes you a jerk, and less ego should, therefore, make you kinder and more thoughtful. With this bias in place, it makes perfect sense that most people who start out on a spiritual path view ego as something undesirable on the path to awareness. As a long-time meditation teacher, I can't tell you how many times I've heard some version of, "My thoughts just won't stop, and I need to get them to stop, right?"

This is a view of *ego as enemy*, something that needs to be overcome, overpowered, or conquered. And right away, we can see an impossible paradox. The mind is at war with itself and the ego wants to quiet the ego. If you've ever sat and tried to quiet your mind, you know the result first-hand: more noise. An effort to contain, change, or control a busy mind may work for a few moments, but before long the mind is racing away again, doing what it does—judging, living in the past or the future, racing around in circles like a donkey tied to a pole. An ego's job, after all, is to be an ego, and that has two important implications. The first is the ego can't overpower itself. The second is that an ego's job is to make sense of the world after first dividing the world into two broad categories: me and not-me.

Junpo used to tell a joke, that an everyday person's thoughts are some version of *memememememememe…you…memememememmemememememe*. And that a spiritual person's thoughts were some version of *me…me…me…me…me…me…you…me…me…me…me*. The joke, of course, is that the only difference is the tempo of the thinking, not of the thoughts themselves.

With an idea that ego *seems to be* in our way, most meditations are designed as a bit of a trick. They give the ego something to do, like count breaths, recite mantras, say prayers, follow instructions into the body, or ten thousand other things. And in giving the mind something to do that is different from what it normally does, there's a slight chance that a practitioner's ego might get a peek into a reality deeper than their own thinking. It's a crack they might slip into for a few moments, a breath, or a heartbeat, but in that moment they may see the world as it is instead of how they shape and mold it with their minds.

This stillness one glimpses isn't something we *find* and *uncover*, however. It's not *out there*, away from us. We don't need to quiet our minds to *find* the stillness. We don't need to *beat* our minds into submission, or to *fight* with ourselves to shut ourselves up. We don't need to *recite* mantras or *count* breaths for decades, hoping to get a glimpse of liberation. In Zen, we don't do any of these tricks to give the mind something to do. We don't fight our thinking at all. In fact, we embrace it.

One way to imagine this is a metaphor: your thoughts as a pack of horses that are high strung and energetic. You could get them into a tiny barn, close them inside, and then try and get a bridle and a saddle on each and every one, but there are hundreds of them, and you're only meditating for thirty minutes. And for every horse you saddle, two more seem to appear. The other approach is to give that pack of horses a nice big open field to run and play in. They can jump, eat, shit, fuck, and do anything else that horses might do if left alone.

If you learn to relate to your mind as a big, empty field to play inside of, your attention can be brought to other parts of you, especially those parts that can watch the thoughts race, turn, jump, and play. You don't try and control the thoughts—that's actually impossible. Instead, you allow the thoughts, and put your focus on that which does the allowing.

This is the subtle and simple shift of Zen, one that allows all to be—all opinions to be, all identities to be, all stories to be, all narratives to be, and all facts to be. We don't rest our attention with the noise, but instead come back to that which can see the noise as an object in its awareness.

With this approach, a busy mind is just more to watch. It's more fuel for your spiritual fire, more of a chance to see through that false narrative of a self and observe *the process that it really is*. Now, on occasion, and with practice, the mind can indeed go quiet. Sometimes profoundly so, and thoughts stop arising for a minute, or two, or ten, or sixty. But that isn't the goal, and if that happens, what do you do? Nothing, of course, but simply watch the now-empty fields with no horses in them whatsoever. Because the horses will come back—they always do. The point is not to have an empty field or a full one, but to allow the field to just be exactly as it is.

The stillness you seek is here, now. You can't find it, or uncover it, or make room for it, or discover it. Those are all just tricks we play to give our ego something to do. No, it's here, now. The stillness is here, now, in this very moment, radiating out from the core of your true self, through your cells, and into the world. All you have to do is realize what's already here. There's a saying in spirituality: "The diamond is in your pocket." And yet we turn over whole houses looking for that diamond, looking everywhere but right in our own pocket pressed right up against the very skin of our own leg.

The German mystic Meister Eckhart said, "God is nearer to me than I am to myself."[20] How is that possible, unless God is already here, fully, waiting to be *allowed* so one can see what is already true and present? From

---

20 From *Meister Eckhart's Sermons*, translated into English by Claud Field, 1909.

this place, prayer is unnecessary, for there is no separation between our mind and the mind of God. But our egos like to do things that are active: discovering, finding, uncovering, capturing, judging, and praying.

Allowing isn't really an ego's thing. Allowing is a foundational Zen practice, which does *not* mean it's an easy practice or one just for beginners. Every spiritual teacher I've ever talked with is always in some kind of ongoing relationship to this foundational teaching, no matter how deep or profound their realization.

When we fully allow, there can be an extraordinary moment when we look out at the world as awareness itself—fully awake, fully present, fully enlightened, full and complete, and utterly free. And not neutral, not passionless, but full of laughter, goodness, and an ease in how we engage with the world. For even as we engage with humor, passion, and incredible heart-fullness, there is nothing to do, and this is utterly, perfectly normal, and not extraordinary in the least. The mind may go quiet for a few minutes, or a few days. But it will start back up again, doing what it does—being dualistic, judgmental, time-bound, neurotic, obsessive, petty, and sometimes grand, loving, powerful, wise, creative, and kind. But we are now something both bigger and smaller, not *just* a self, and not even *just a process*, and no longer as attached to those stories we tell ourselves about ourselves. Liberation comes within the world and not outside of it, and it's hardly realistic to expect that the deepest spiritual realizations cause thinking to stop entirely. But our relationship to that thinking is radially, forever altered.

Egos don't awaken. Egos *can't* awaken. They only can be informed by and transformed by the awakened view. They're also not the enemy, something that you need to overcome in order to *discover* what's *there*. You just need to *allow* what's *here*.

Once on a retreat I was attending, a student (he was, in fact, a good friend of mine who had just been through a bruising breakup) asked Junpo: "Who awakens?"

Junpo threw his head back and laughed.

"Who indeed," he said, cocking an eyebrow. "It's a *great* question. A *great* koan. You can sit with it this week, my brother.[21]

As we move forward with this book, you will more deeply explore how to choose awakening, because you'll have a more solid sense of what that *does* and *does not* mean. Remember that enlightenment is liberation within life, not from it.

---

21 Eventually Junpo told him, "You don't awaken. Awakening awakens!"

CHAPTER 4

When the Buddha Needs Therapy

Junpo used to glare at his students in a mock serious expression: "Japanese Zen is the *perfect* vehicle to totally and completely awaken you in every way." He would pause, letting the audience take the bait, with many nodding their heads in agreement. And then he would add with a wry smile, "...*for* eighteenth century Japan." People would gape at him, and he'd laugh. "Japanese Zen is xenophobic, racist, sexist, autocratic, emotionally repressed, and close-minded. In other words, perfect for a Japanese man living in 1725. But not so perfect for us today." As was often the case with his talks, the audience would be confused and unsure why a Zen master was knocking the legs out from under his own lineage.

In traditional Zen, anytime you have an emotional reaction of any kind, you're told to "go back to the Zendo." In other words, to keep meditating until you transcend the emotional mind altogether. And in Japan, 150 years before any understanding of Western psychology and the unconscious, sexual drives, repressed emotionality, childhood trauma, attachment styles, personality types, cultural conditioning, and psychopathology, there was no understanding of emotional reality in the way we have it today.

Even modern Zen will train a student to develop tremendous mindfulness, and they'll be able to see as awareness catches sensations and emotions arising. They will be able to sit in this awareness and choose to be non-reactive to anything their mind throws their way. In other words, they will still get activated in traffic, or when their mother calls, or when someone is late to a meeting, or walks too slowly on the sidewalk. The trigger, the activation point, remains, but they develop a capacity to "go around" it and let it arise and fall away without reacting. This is sometimes what is meant by spiritual bypassing—going around emotional content rather than allowing yourself to fully feel it and explore it, because in so doing you risk becoming it.

A Zen student would be scolded for becoming angry, but not for having the impulse to get angry every single day at the same thing. I've known more than one Zen student to respond to this reality by simply changing the routine of their life so they can avoid the trigger. Mom make you mad? Stop taking her calls. Intimate relationships bring up fear? Move to a monastery and become a celibate. Can't stand social media? Close all your accounts. This hardly seems a path for growth and self-discovery, but perhaps it is better than pilling with more reactivity. (Don't we have enough of that in our world?) But before we talk about the problems with bypassing, consider this: If most of the world had just this capacity to avoid and bypass, the world would largely see an end to the major causes of conflict. Let that sink in for a moment, especially when you're in a place like Boulder, Colorado, where I live, and where some people dismiss spiritual bypassing as a sin just slightly less offensive than Nazism.

It's impractical to live your life avoiding triggers, of course, but much more importantly, the triggers are the key to your awakening. That was another of Junpo's insights: Your angst is your liberation. After he was made a Zen roshi at fifty years of age after six years of living in the monastery, he made his own curious choice. Most people would, at that age, simply start teaching and transmitting what they'd learned. But he didn't. He ended up moving from New York to Boulder and beginning a long period of intense psychological shadow work. I don't know of any other teacher who did that, and so I asked him why. The answer was recorded in our book, *The Heart of Zen:*

"Because," he said, with a smile, "I was a fraud. There was nowhere to hide. In 1992, when recognized as a so-called Zen master, I had to face the fact that in my case Zen was just not working effectively—not for me or for many others. I had insight but I wasn't free. I had a lot of psychological damage from my upbringing, and Zen simply hadn't touched it. I could transcend it, true, control it with my will, but the damage was still intact and mostly untouched. I didn't know if that was just my problem, or if it was something that was common in the larger Buddhist community. I saw, with my six years in the monastery, a lot of psychological shadows in myself, but also in the men and women training with me, in other spiritual communities, and in Eido Shimano himself [Junpo's teacher and the head abbot of the monastery]. But how widespread it was, and what it meant, I could only guess at.

… How come after decades of practice, real wisdom and compassion were not ruling my life, directing my behavior, and transforming lust, violent anger, jealousy, envy? How could love and compassion not hold in the face of my internal conflict? I could remain non-reactive in the face of these things, mind you, but it was a very repressive energy that was required. And my negative emotions still flourished, and they would sometimes overpower my discipline and my insight. Why? How? I had to know."

THE PROBLEM WITH ZEN AND PSYCHOTHERAPY

The problem with Zen, therefore, is that it can make you rigid and calcified, and out of touch with your emotions. Instead of learning to be in touch with what you're feeling, you're only in touch with what you're feeling *so you can get away from it and around it*. This model worked well for the many centuries that humankind had no real understanding of psychology, but the twentieth century showed us some of the problems with traditional Zen training.

Therapy and psychoanalysis are powerful tools that everyone should try *at least* a few times in their lives. All of us, without exception, have blind spots created by our childhood experiences, our culture, and our limiting beliefs that directly impact how we see the world, how we are in relationships, and how we manage the nuts and bolts of our lives. If you don't think this applies to you, that means it's *especially* true for you. As we've already covered, much of the free will you think you have is, in fact, conditioned, and therapy can go a long way in helping you understand the places where you're asleep at the wheel of your life but think you're fully in charge.

With that said, there's also a gap in therapy. If you're seeking to find eternal happiness or somehow get away from yourself through therapy, you will find that no matter how far you go, how deep you dig, there's always another trauma, another wound, another repression in the mind and body. People can become addicted to therapy and to the attention they put on themselves, forever trying to fix something that isn't necessarily so much broken as it is human and fallible. If you've been in therapy for twenty years and are still unable to cope without it, something might be wrong either with your therapist or with how you're holding the therapy.

The problem with meditation is that it cannot awaken your shadows, no matter how hard you meditate or how deeply you awaken otherwise. Genuinely enlightened teachers can have tremendously deep spiritual insight while also suffering from very deep psychological shadows. The idea is that *what is in shadow is in shadow*, meaning it can't be seen with your conscious mind, nor can it be seen by awareness itself, at least as far as I've been able to tell. This helps to explain how some of the truly great spiritual teachers have done truly human and seemingly unethical things, from power grabs and psychological manipulation, to sexual abuse and embezzlement.

Therapy can't free you from yourself or help you to face fully what lies within. Meditation can't awaken you to your childhood wounding or the deepest and most neurotic parts of your conditioned self. This was all said much more succinctly by Junpo: "The only trouble with Zen and with psychotherapy is that they don't work."

Used together, however, they can create powerful and lasting transformation inside of us.

TRAUMA: A SPECIAL CASE

We all tend to think of traumatized people as having suffered severe abuse, war, rape, or some other horrific circumstance. Yet the truth is far more shocking. Nearly all of us have some residue of trauma in our bodies.[22] A traumatic event can get stored in our body at any time without us knowing it. This includes things we carry over from our childhoods, but also things that happen to us as adults, like surgeries, divorces, job loss, the death of a loved one or even a loved pet, poverty, and challenging experiences with psychedelic drugs, just to name a few.

A caveat: I am not a trauma specialist, medical doctor, or psychologist, and interested readers would do well to investigate some of the books in the footnotes of this chapter and seek out more authoritative viewpoints than my own. Trauma is a rich and complex field, and more is being learned about it every single year. This section is simply designed to give you an overview of trauma and why it matters on your spiritual journey.[23]

Trauma happens when we can't soothe ourselves during or after an experience—when we can't regulate our nervous system and get overwhelmed by it. The experience then gets "stored" in the body-mind and remains there until we can fully experience it. It is obviously easier to get emotionally overwhelmed as children, which is why childhood trauma is more common than adult trauma. Being alone and sick as a child, for instance, tends to be much more frightening than being alone and sick as an adult. Yet veterans, first responders, and those in abusive relationships can experience significant trauma as adults, as can victims of physical or emotional violence.

I'm going to take a risk here and say that if you're reading this, it is very likely that you have some unprocessed trauma in your body-mind right now.

---

[22] Bessel van der Kolk, *The Body Keeps the Score: Brain, Mind, and Body in the Transformation of Trauma* (London: Penguin Books, 2015).

[23] Bessel van der Kolk, *The Body Keeps the Score: Brain, Mind, and Body in the Transformation of Trauma* (London: Penguin Books, 2015).
- *Gabor Maté, In the Realm of Hungry Ghosts: Close Encounters with Addiction (Berkeley, CA: North Atlantic Books, 2010).*
- *Diane Poole Heller, The Power of Attachment: How to Create Deep and Lasting Intimate Relationships (Boulder, CO: Sounds True, 2019).*
- *Don Barlow, Recovery from Complex PTSD (Barlow Wellness Publications, 2021).*

I've yet to meet a human being who doesn't. Understanding trauma means we need to take a drive-by of our physical brains to better understand what's happening on a biological level.

Humans have a three-part brain sometimes called the *triune brain*. We have our most basic brain, the autonomic nervous system, which regulates heart and breath and all the unconscious functions of the body, as well as our basic survival. We also have a limbic brain, which allows for emotion. And we have a cortex, which makes us uniquely human and houses all of our thoughts and ideas and beliefs. When humans regulate our system, it's from the "top down," with our cortex regulating the other two brains. When we're children, the cortex is still growing, which is why it's important for adults to help regulate a child's nervous system, because they basically cannot do so themselves. This makes us much more prone to being traumatized as children. If you look at videos of baby mammals, like elephants, experiencing something traumatic like a lioness attack, you'll see an adult rush over and "console" the baby, helping them to regulate their nervous system. The baby mammal may shake and make noise and discharge the energy until its nervous system comes back to what is called baseline, or a normal resting place.

As adult humans, our cortex reigns in both the limbic system and autonomic nervous system in obvious ways. We might get angry at our boss but not punch him in the face, which is the cortex doing its job and remembering there are consequences for doing something like that. Or we might walk around a corner and find a friend standing there unexpectedly and jump, but then laugh at ourselves for the overreaction. When we are regulated, our cortex can put what's happening into context, so the more primitive parts of our brain go from being activated to being relaxed. And we can come back to baseline.

Dysregulation happens when the autonomic nervous system takes over in something like a panic attack, or the limbic system takes over in something like deep feelings of anxiety or depression. When we're in a dysregulated state, our cortex gets hijacked and is unable to regulate the lower brains. And the cortex itself might get taken over by the lower brains. For instance, in a road-rage attack, we feel calm as we follow the guy who pissed us off for ten miles, only to cut him off and start the whole process over again. That is hardly the cortex working at its highest. Or we might rationalize free-floating anxiety by using our cortex to subscribe to scary-sounding conspiracies we find online, justifying and rationalizing an internal fear based on a perceived external tormentor.

There's no talking about trauma without talking about the *amygdala*, an ancient part of the brain. This is the home of the fight or flight response and, most importantly, to our personal spectrum of fight or flight (I'll get into that shortly). Most of our sensory information is processed through the amygdala, so our sight, smell, hearing, taste, and sensation all filter through this part of the brain before they get processed by either the limbic brain or the cortex.

Think about that: Everything you're experiencing in and around you right now that is a sensation is first going through one of the oldest parts of your brain, before those impulses are processed by your feeling or thinking brains. This is for obvious evolutionary purposes—if we see a tiger or a rockslide, the amygdala will take control of us and literally move us into action before we have a single thought or feeling. If you see a bear and run, you do not think, "Oh shit, that's a bear and I'd better run because I'm now feeling fear!" You just run, and afterward those thoughts and that feeling arises and you impose them into your memory of what happened.[24] This amazing evolutionary adaptation helped us survive very dangerous times over many tens of thousands of years.

The amygdala associates dangerous experiences with events, which makes perfect sense. If you see a tiger in a particular part of the forest at a particular time of day, you will very much remember to be careful the next time you're there. If you hear a rattlesnake and get bitten, you will forever associate that unforgettable rattle with danger and with pain. The amygdala pairs painful experiences with actual events in our lives, and then the brain hardwires that connection so we can react very, very quickly in the future.

---

24 Peter Levine, *Waking the Tiger: Healing Trauma* (Berkeley, CA: North Atlantic Books, 1997).

This paring is key to understanding one of the ways we are, as Junpo said, almost entirely conditioned beings. If you were bitten by a dog as a child, your amygdala will pair dogs with danger. It's likely you will carry an intense fear of dogs as an adult (if you weren't able to regulate the experience when it happened with the help of an adult). If you were neglected or abused by your mother, you might carry distrust of women your entire life. If as a boy you were bullied by other boys, you might distrust groups of men as an adult. And there can be odder associations as well. As a child I had numerous, painful experiences at the dentist's office, and to this day the particular smell of a dentist's office will cause strong anxiety to arise in anticipation of impending pain.

The amygdala has one job, and that's to keep us alive, and one of the most important ways it does this is by pairing seemingly existential threats with past events, so it can be vigilant for anything that resembles a threat. The problem, of course, is that the pairing is very imprecise and it's adapted to life-and-death threats, not the more mundane ones we typically experience in our modern life. My life was never in danger at the dentist's office, but my amygdala doesn't know that. The amygdala's job isn't to be smart. It's to be vigilant.

A SPECTRUM OF FIGHT OR FLIGHT

You can think of our autonomic nervous system as having a range. On the upper side, there's arousal, known as sympathetic activation. On the lower side, there's relaxation, known as parasympathetic activation. We don't want to be fully in one state or the other—to be aroused all the time would mean anxiousness and panic as a nearly constant state. To be in fully parasympathetic activation would be no better, for we'd be mostly numbed out to anything that happened to us in life and never swerve to avoid a pedestrian who stepped suddenly into our lane.

When we're well-regulated, a car might swerve into our lane and we will react and swerve out of the way. But within a few moments, or within minutes at the most, we'll be back to our baseline—feeling fine, maybe even smiling a little at how scared we were. But if we're not well-regulated, we may remain in a hypervigilant state for much longer, maybe having to pull over to the side of the road, or perhaps, hours later, breaking into tears or needing to have a few stiff drinks in order to get our cortex "on top of" the activation.

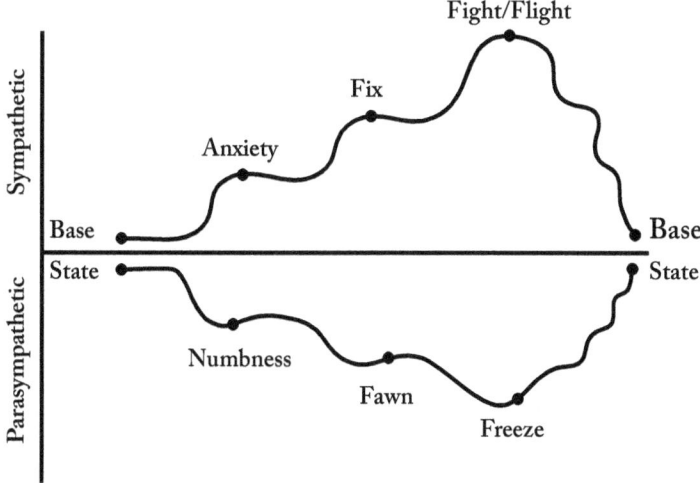

Fight or flight is the home of the autonomic nervous system's sympathetic activation. We all know these states and have all experienced them at some point. Full sympathetic activation means our amygdala literally takes control of us and we either literally fight or literally run, all before we have a single thought. Think of a friend jumping out from behind a corner to scare you—there's just your response, before you think or feel anything. Yet we also know the "deer in the headlights" response, when we just freeze in response to something. Someone jumps out from behind a corner and we can't move for a moment. This is the same extreme reaction as fight or flight, but it happens on the other side of the spectrum, at the far end of the parasympathetic response. We freeze rather than go to fight/flight. (See the accompanying graph.)

To state the obvious, there's not much we can choose to do when we have a full-blown fight/flight/freeze response, because the amygdala highjacks the whole brain and therefore the whole body. Fortunately, this is usually only for a moment before the limbic system and the cortex come back. But fight, flight, freeze, and full relaxation exist on a spectrum. Between them are semi-activated states. If we move away from full-on fight/flight/freeze, we'll find "mildly activated" states, sometimes called "fix or fawn" responses. These are places where we can bring awareness and choice because the cortex is still working—just not well. In the next chapter, I'll explain how meditation can help you to find the choice point in this "mildly activated" state.

Before that, however, I want to tell the story of two men, Paul and Dave. They both had overbearing mothers who dominated their childhoods, told them how to dress and who could be their friends, and tried to force them into careers the young men didn't really want because they were the safest and most prestigious careers their mothers saw. Paul grows up, grinds through his job, and marries a woman who is very self-assured—although his friends think she's domineering. When there's conflict in the marriage and Paul's wife gets upset, he tends to shut down and do what she wants, even though deep down he feels a bit ashamed and wishes he could better stand up for himself. He avoids activities his wife thinks are dangerous, doesn't associate with women his wife thinks are attractive, and tries to keep her happy and contented.

Dave, on the other hand, never married. He ended up dropping out of college and taking a job as a bartender, a job his mother hated. He tends to date women who are hard to get close to, and he has a hard time with any real emotional vulnerability. More than one woman has accused Dave of being a Peter Pan, or a man who refuses to grow up and take responsibility for his own life. When Dave feels a woman is trying to control him, he speaks quickly and sharply and doesn't, in his words, "take any shit," and soon afterward he ends the relationship.

When Paul is confronted, he doesn't go into a freeze response, standing in his kitchen frozen as his wife snaps at him for coming home late. Instead, he goes into "fawn" mode, which means there is activation in his amygdala and of his autonomic nervous system, but the activation isn't overwhelming. His limbic system and his cortex are still working, but not as well. He will "fawn" for safety, or perhaps try and placate his wife and apologize and make excuses rather than say what's really on his mind, which maybe was something like, "I'm literally only four minutes late," or, "I'm sorry I'm a little late. Can we let it go and just say hi to each other?"

Dave, on the other hand, when confronted with the exact same scenario, has the exact same brain response, except his brain goes into the sympathetic rather than parasympathetic reaction. He responds by "mansplaining" and trying to "fix" the problem. "Look, he says, "I'm a little late. Come on. There was traffic. And you were five minutes late yesterday. How dare you stand there and give me shit for something you did! Jesus, what a fucking hypocrite!"

For all humans, once we get "aroused" by something, our brains kick into the higher sympathetic or parasympathetic states to deal with stressors or perceived threats. When we add this into the amygdala's pairing response, we can see how our brains can get high-jacked from "underneath" in an attempt to keep us safe. If Dave's girlfriend argues back with him, he might move into a full-on fight response and start to yell. If Paul's wife pushes back against him and snaps, he might slow even further down and start to feel foggy and numb and just feel like he's "collapsed" in plain sight, giving into a full-on freeze response.

We are saddled, perhaps gifted, with brains designed to work best in a far more violent and dangerous world. We have all been slaves to the power of the more primitive and older parts of our brain high-jacking our cortex and removing our capacity to have choice. We see shades of this anytime we get "triggered" and it seems like we get "taken over" by some very reactive, and very emotional, part of ourselves. It's like we lose our capacity to choose what we really want to say, and how we really want to react, which we do. This is part of our conditioned response, but there is hope.

THE HYSTERICAL-HISTORICAL

Biological conditioning is powerful because of pairing, and how the amygdala pairs a fight/flight/freeze response with a specific event.

When we get even mildly traumatized as children or as adults, the "pairing" circuits in the brain become deeply wired to fire quickly in certain circumstances, bypassing the neocortex so that the threat can be addressed quickly. We might go into fight/flight/freeze or into fix/fawn, but we're taken somewhere we don't choose to go. The trouble is when we're not *really* in danger, this paired response creates the opposite of what we want. Rather than getting understanding and closeness and attunement, we get conflict or isolation, or anger or dissociation.

Junpo defined our "hysterical-historical" places as those where we're likely to fly off the handle quickly and without thinking. It's where our conditioning is the strongest. Dave goes to fight or fix, and Paul to freeze or fawn, even though both men had very similar mothers. Yet each man has a hysterical-historical that causes them to *react* to the women in their lives, rather than to *choose* a compassionate, intelligent response. Both Dave and Paul want close and intimate connection, but both have been so strongly affected by their childhood experience of conditional love that they're imprisoned by that conditioning.

Perhaps one day Paul gets tired of always putting his wife's needs before his own, and for never standing up for what he really wants. Moreover, he gets tired of how he is unable to skillfully and lovingly stand up to her, to let her know that he's being slightly "smothered," not only by how she's behaving, *but in how he's responding*. After all, he's not a just a victim here, but is *allowing* and *contributing to* the dynamic. And one day perhaps Dave gets tired of being alone, and seeing more than one amazing woman leave his life so that he can maintain some sense of "freedom." Dave starts to see that he really wants to find someone who he can go deep and grow old with, someone who knows him as well as he knows her. And in the deepest part of his heart, he begins to see how he's avoided intimacy.

In the book, *The Body Keeps the Score*, the Boston-based Dutch psychiatrist and PTSD researcher Bessel van der Kolk explores the disconnection between the body and the mind that trauma creates. He says:

> One does not have be a combat soldier, or visit a refugee camp in Syria or the Congo to encounter trauma. Trauma happens to us, our friends, our families, and our neighbors. Research by the Centers for Disease Control and Prevention has shown that one in five Americans was sexually molested as a child; one in four was beaten by a parent to the point of a mark being left on their body; and one in three

couples engages in physical violence. A quarter of us grew up with alcoholic relatives, and one out of eight witnessed their mother being beaten or hit.

My own childhood could be very, very loving, but also very emotionally intense. I was raised in a maternal home where alcohol flowed far too freely. When my mother was an infant, in 1939, she was in a pediatric ICU with pneumonia before antibiotics were used to treat bacterial infections—and largely left to herself for the first year of her life. This is now known to be the potential cause of a myriad of mental health problems.[25] My father was the eighth of nine children born into the Depression-era South in 1936, and his upbringing was one of abject poverty with no running water, electricity, or indoor plumbing of any kind. Three of his siblings died as children. As he grew up, three boys were packed into a single bed, and there was often no food to eat. (And I don't mean "not enough" food, but literally *no* food).

My childhood home was filled with the belief that the world was, at its core, a cruel and dangerous place and that a man needed to be hard and ready to meet it. It could be a loving home as well, and there are plenty of happy and wonderful memories of love and care shown to me. It is important that those experiences not be negated, for my parents could be generous and incredibly warm and kind—reading books and singing songs as I fell asleep, and encouraging me, as a young adult, to follow my dream of being a professional writer. As I've gotten older, I've come to greatly appreciate and deeply value all the things that were loving and good about my childhood, yet I first had to clean up the parts that were messier.

---

25 • https://www.nature.com/articles/s41372-018-0282-9
  • https://academic.oup.com/jpepsy/article-abstract/46/7/814/6303584v
  • https://www.mayoclinic.org/diseases-conditions/reactive-attachment-disorder/symptoms-causes/syc-20352939
  • https://www.aacap.org/AACAP/Families_and_Youth/Facts_for_Families/FFF-Guide/Attachment-Disorders-085.aspx

As a very sensitive and highly intelligent child who was introverted and inward-looking, I was almost the opposite of what my mother imagined was necessary to survive in the hard world she saw as real. She did what she thought was necessary to stamp out the vulnerability, introspection, quietness, and shyness that she perceived as flaws or weaknesses in my character.

Spankings weren't uncommon, nor were threats of using a wooden spoon or a meat tenderizer—my brother and I had to choose which one was to be used. Love could seem largely conditional on me not being myself, and I faced a steady torrent of reasons why I was not okay as I was. On top of that, I went to a corporal punishment, all-boys Catholic school where, if we were caught doing something wrong, we were forced to kneel on sidewalks with books stacked on our upturned hands until we said, "Mercy." I was backhanded out of chairs, shoved up against walls, isolated and publicly shamed for my growing defiance, and once nearly choked unconscious with a forearm for not having my tie worn properly. Love and violence were equally capricious and seemed independent of any external logic, and it was hard to tell which one might meet me on any given day.

By the time I reached my early teens, I had become a hard and angry young man. It seemed like everyone was telling me that I wasn't extroverted enough, athletic enough, pious enough, respectful enough, achievement-oriented enough, confident enough, studious enough, or well-groomed enough. But I had become more than tough enough for any adult who dared face me.

I learned to lock my sensitivity, intelligence, and curiosity inside of me where it could never be seen or abused again. The entire world had become a place of danger, especially from anyone who attempted to hold authority of any kind over me. The unpredictable emotions of my mother caused me to become aloof and distrust emotionality of any kind, except anger. I developed a deeply anti-authoritarian streak that nearly got me kicked out of school on multiple occasions, and landed me in jail three times before my eighteenth birthday. I smoked cigarettes and cannabis and drank alcohol, starting at thirteen years of age.

The sum total of these experiences left a deep impact on me and my capacity to be in relationships in ways that I actually wanted (with vulnerability, honesty, and a deep emotional connection), and it's taken many years of therapeutic work to understand, transform, and integrate the complexity of my childhood. And the work continues.

Junpo was raised in a violent alcoholic household where he and his brothers were regularly beaten by his father. They were not protected by his mother, who his father never touched. (His childhood experiences are covered extensively in my book of Junpo's life, *A Heart Blown Open*.) As he explored these shadows starting in his early fifties, he was astounded at how much his seemingly-free behavior was, in fact, deeply conditioned by his childhood.

Van der Kolk:
It takes tremendous energy to keep functioning while carrying the memory of terror, and the shame of utter weakness and vulnerability.

Junpo made peace with his parents long before they, or he, died. My parents and I are now very close, and have been for many years. Yet the past lives on in my brain and is a source of continual work and awareness for me, a source of tremendous understanding and self-awareness, and a place to find an endless well of humility for my humanness.

Van der Kolk:
The brain-disease model overlooks four fundamental truths: (1) our capacity to destroy one another is matched by our capacity to heal one another. Restoring relationships and community is central to restoring well-being; (2) language gives us the power to change ourselves and others by communicating our experiences, helping us to define what we know, and finding a common sense of meaning; (3) we have the ability to regulate our own physiology, including some of the so-called involuntary functions of the body and brain, through such basic activities as breathing, moving, and touching; and (4) we can change social conditions to create environments in which children and adults can feel safe and where they can thrive.

How do you overcome this conditioning? It takes four steps. First, you need to make your conditioning conscious. You need to realize and admit that you have conditioned reactions in you that are, in essence, not yours. They were *put into you*.

Second, you need to notice when and where those conditioned actions arise. Meditation helps us to slow the mind down, so that what seems to happen in a split second can stretch out because we have developed a witnessing capacity in the mind.

Third, you need to have someone reflect to you what they see, and to help you to monitor your progress and your ability to see into some of these "shadows" in your psyche. Therapy is very helpful and necessary for this.

And fourth, you need to be *able* and *willing* to make another choice when a triggering event happens.

The patterns of how we think when we feel "triggered," no matter if we're conscious of it or not, are deeply worn into the brain. Our hypothetical men, Dave and Paul, and our real men, Junpo and Keith, all need to do the same thing: realize there's a pattern, slow the reactive process down, get some outside help to see the patterns for ourselves, notice there's a choice point, and make a different choice. If we can't make a choice here, we certainly will never be able to choose enlightenment. I'll explain exactly why that's the case in the following chapter.

OUR INTOLERABLE SITUATION

Underneath the flight/flight/free and fawn/fix is the fear of being exposed to something that we find intolerable. This intolerable thing is almost always tied either to childhood trauma, adult trauma, or both.

All of us have something in our lives that we find just *intolerable*. For some, it's infidelity or lack of trust. For others it might be dishonesty. Others, integrity. Or lack of loyalty or sexual intimacy, or challenges to one's authority. It could be displays of emotional intensity from a man or a woman. Or maybe hypocrites drive you crazy, or stupid people, or selfish leaders. Know-it-alls, mansplainers, or woke idealists. Republicans, QAnoners, NRA members, or opinioned people of any stripe. But no matter what it is, it's the place in our lives where we seem to have no ability to do anything but react. In other words, something in our autonomic nervous system and our fight/flight/freeze or fix/fawn response is getting triggered. Most of us never see our reactivity happening in certain circumstances and might only notice it after the fact, or after someone close to us points out a pattern of behavior. Our rationalizations for our reactivity are real enough to us, but hardly true for anyone not standing in our shoes.

Doshin MJ Nelson Roshi of Integral Zen, one of Junpo's Dharma heirs, was the first person I heard speaking about the idea of the intolerable situation. When working with a new person, he'd ask a simple question: "What is it in life you just can't stand? What's the thing that just drives you bananas?" And people would, every single time, tell him. It was like a key to the door of their own personal trauma. After all, people love to tell you the things they find intolerable, usually presuming that you share their feelings because it's so obvious how awful it is (whatever *it* may be).

For many years, I didn't think I really had an intolerable situation. Some things made me mad, especially some of my intimate relationships, but I didn't think that this whole "intolerable" thing fit me. I was a cool and detached guy. I thought I liked to keep people a little distant from me, friends close but not too close, show some emotion but not too much. "It's like you have a protected, inner core that no one can touch," one girlfriend noted. I said nothing, but did think, *Of course I have a protected, inner core. Why would I, or anyone, not?* Hiding the core of my being was a perfectly rational choice to me.

I was once engaged to a very dynamic and accomplished woman, but after some years together we started to have all kinds of problems with intimacy—emotional, sexual, even verbal. My needs weren't getting met (nor hers, different from mine) and we did many hours of couples therapy, got support from wise friends, and sought counsel from our spiritual teachers, all to no avail. In the end, I began having a series of sexual and emotional affairs, getting my needs met in secret. When I finally came clean with what I had done, the pain I caused her was nearly indescribable. Nothing she did justified or excused my behavior, which I alone own and am responsible for.

We were in a dynamic, absolutely, and that dynamic was based on our mutually shared wounding, blind spots, and conditioned patterns.

Those things *seemed to leave me no choice* but to cheat, and my rationalizations told me as much. Of course, my choice was there all along, and radically so. It was an unhealthy relationship because our childhood wounds were so perfectly matched up to one another—so much so that one night we came to our house and I sat in the car, looking at the front entrance. "I don't really want to go inside," I admitted. "I feel like I'm back at home. At my parents' house, and I'm like a teenager again or something." Astoundingly, she said, "I feel the same way." We had recreated the worst parts of our childhood homes because, on some level, it was what we knew—to be home and to not be able to be ourselves, either one of us. This is what Junpo meant when he said we were almost entirely conditioned, more like Pavlov's dogs than human beings.

I didn't know it then, but found out later that my intolerable situation is vulnerability. I learned to repress the need for maternal care and stand up to my mother regardless of how badly I might be hurting or needing someone to love me. My Christian educators showed their love of God and their depth of caring through physical abuse, along with dogma and punishment. The lesson I learned was vulnerability, and its expressions were the most dangerous things in the world. My needs for intimacy, if I dared to have any, were best met in secret and in shadow where I was least likely to get hurt. This was how I unconsciously lived my life from my early teens until my early forties. It took years of men's work, therapy, meditation, intense work with Junpo Roshi and Doshin Roshi, and even things as controversial as ketamine-based psychotherapy[26] to help me see some of my own conditioning and to find the places where I had choice.

---

26 According the Sage Institute (https://sageinst.org/kat): "Ketamine-assisted therapy (KAT) is a unique therapeutic method used to address a variety of mental health conditions, including depression, post-traumatic stress, chronic pain, addiction, and some forms of anxiety. It involves the use of ketamine to enhance and deepen the therapeutic process, and the use of psychotherapy and other integrative forms of treatment to amplify and prolong the curative effects of ketamine."

As Van der Kolk said, "Our capacity to destroy one another is matched by our capacity to heal one another. Restoring relationships and community is central to restoring well-being." I had been alone as far back as I could remember. Even when I was with my friends or my former fiancée, I was still alone, because I couldn't bear the thought of "burdening" them with my self-perceived weakness and softness and whining about myself. Because that would be vulnerable, and vulnerability was intolerable to me. The wounds of childhood sat, untouched, impacting my capacity to love and to be loved and making me an at-times terrible partner in intimate relationships, a man who hid, proudly, inside of the castle of himself.

When we react instead of choosing our response, we end up more alone, more isolated, and more afraid than before.

No matter what our intolerable situation is, no matter what it is that triggers us to act out or collapse, we always want the same thing: to be seen and heard; to connect with others; to have our fear and vulnerability held so we don't have to hold it for ourselves; and for someone to remind us that we're not alone and that we were never alone even though life can seem sometimes unbearably so.

Take a moment to imagine you at your very worst, no matter what that is for you. Maybe it's screaming at the guy who cut you off in traffic, or actually kicking your dog, or allowing a boss to harass and verbally intimate you while you collapse into self-hatred. Maybe it's driving drunk, or looking at porn, or something that society would deem dark and dangerous. Imagine you doing that thing and imagine being met with love and understanding and care and empathy *in that place*. What might happen to you then? What might emerge to be seen, and possibly healed? What might that do to your hysterical-historical?

CHAPTER 5

No One Has Ever Made You Angry (Really)

We've covered the three poisons of the mind in traditional Zen: attachment, ignorance, and aversion. Attachment to things like our identity, our opinions, our valuations, and our ideas of what's right and wrong are directly related to our suffering and the possibility of war, be it inside of our own heads or between families, lovers, or countries. As I said before, we don't go to war over ideologies but over our *attachment* to those ideologies.

When we hold our opinions of things lightly, and we look to be discerning rather than judgmental, we can observe that it's raining outside, that my partner seems especially moody, and that we don't appear to be doing enough to address climate change. Or I can judge the stupid fucking rain outside, hate that bitch of a partner and her irrational moods, and wonder how so many stupid people can be doing so many stupid things to ruin the planet.

One perspective invites curiosity and an openness to dialog and change, the other is the prelude to war. You might be correct in your discernment of the world or the people in it, but your *attachment* to that discernment, known as judgment, fuels internal and external division. Remember that you cannot be liberated and opinioned at the same time, but you can be liberated and discerning. *Opinioned and enlightened* are mutually exclusive states of being. When you know something in your being, as opposed to just your mind, you don't need to argue about it or defend it with self-righteousness, attack, vitriol, contempt, shaming, and derision.

With respect to ignorance, the second of the three poisons, I have offered the fact that *we are what we seek*—and that there is no practice, no work, no form of meditation that can allow you to find something that you already have. Ignorance of this truth sends most practitioners seeking spirituality far away from themselves, sometimes literally to the top of a great mountain where they believe some wise person holds something sacred for them. We seek a great teacher, a great monastery, a great book, even a great online course. Our ignorance of our true nature sends us to thousands upon thousands of places to find that which we already possess. We cannot find enlightenment because it is what we are. The only "work" we can do is that which allows ourselves to *rest in what's here*. A good teacher can help us to see this and experience this for ourselves, and might be a vital part of the path, for good teachers can be good at showing us when we're full of shit or our insight is just an egoic one.

When Junpo was in Japan, many years ago, he was speaking to a Rinzai Zen bishop, who asked him why he was so devoted to his teacher, Eido Shimano Roshi. Junpo gave his answer, which was that Eido meditated all the time. The bishop laughed. "Ha! Because he *has* to! You Americans," he said, "why do you worship your teachers? Here in Japan we look at roshis like good plumbers. They help to fix a problem. Nothing more."

From an ego perspective, the idea you have what you seek can be terrifying. It means no one can rescue you from yourself, for one. And secondly, it means you can't *do* anything to *find* or *capture* or *discover* enlightenment—all action verbs that give an ego something to do. There is only surrender, which, from a genuinely spiritual view, is liberating, but which can be terrifying from an egoic view. To avoid the poison of ignorance, you simply allow yourself to practice *as if* you have what you seek and you merely need to *allow* it to come through you. This cuts out the need for gurus and cults and special tulkus and rinpoches and roshis. The responsibility for spiritual awakening lies fully in the only place it can be: with you. And still, a teacher can be invaluable in helping you to realize this, the same way a plumber can be invaluable in helping you get the shit out of your pipes. But the plumber doesn't cause the pipes to work—he just removes the obstacles so the pipes can be pipes.

The third poison of the mind is aversion, which we'll explore now.

FEELINGS AS INFORMATION

One of the core teachings of Junpo was that feelings are information, no different than our other five senses. When we avoid the information in our feelings, we suffer from aversion.

Sound, taste, hearing, sensation, and sight all arise inside of awareness without us having to do anything at all. As we've learned, these five senses are first *processed* by our amygdala, which has important implications for pairing with events in our life story and making us far more prone to getting "taken over" by some kind of amygdala response, which includes the full spectrum of the sympathetic and parasympathetic nervous system. And yet, before they reach the amygdala they must arise, first, in our awareness. I'll come back to this truth a bit later in this chapter, for the fact that sensations first arise in awareness has profound implication for how we can choose enlightenment, and that's both simpler and more complicated than it sounds.

There are two kinds of information in our feelings. One is when we go into a full amygdala highjack, and our body and brain are literally taken over by our autonomic nervous system, and we go into fight/flight or freeze. The information here is pretty straightforward: We experienced deep fear and deep vulnerability, which is what caused the amygdala to take over our body and mind.

The second kind is when we have a partial amygdala response or a simple limbic brain reaction to the experience of being human, otherwise known as our feelings. We'll start here.

THE TRUTH OF ANGER

There are very few times when one can make a categorical statement that is true all the time, in all places, and in all times. This is one of them. *No one has ever gotten angry who didn't care first.* Anger can only arise when you care about something that has been violated in some way, even if it's just in your imagination. It might be the space in front of your car on a highway, your perceived level of respect from your boss, your love of your country, or your love of your kids. Even the clearly mentally ill person shouting on the corner cares about the topic of his rant.

Anger only ever arises because there is care first. Which means the first thing to arise, before anger, is caring. First caring, and then we make the conscious or unconscious choice for anger. That is kind of amazing if you think about it, because how often do you feel the deep care driving your anger? Probably not very often, at least in the moment, although sometimes in hindsight the care can be clearly seen.

The trouble with anger is that it's messy, noisy, and often counterproductive. We have a saying in martial arts: *An angry warrior is a dead warrior.* I can't tell you how many times in my Kung Fu school I've been sparring my students and watched them get angry. When this happens it is then very, very easy to beat them for the simple reason that anger is messy and imprecise. It isn't relational. It can't listen. It's closed and hard.

When we get angry, our amygdala produces fight or flight hormones such as cortisol and adrenaline. This raises the pulse, narrows the field of vision, lowers blood flow to the neocortex, and puts more blood into the limbs. It makes us, in short, dumber and stronger. Against a trained fighter, uncontrolled anger is as obvious and as effective as a four-year-old having a temper tantrum. You literally see the "lights go out" in their eyes as their consciousness dims. And in you swoop to take them off their feet.

Yet it's not much different outside of the ring. Anger is allowing ourselves to be taken away from what's present on a deeper level—care, and maybe some fear or vulnerability.

It's worth taking stock of how well our anger has served us. We might be angry about the state of the environment, or what our spouse said to us last night, or about being skipped over for the raise. Can you name the times your anger has made things better and gotten you more of what you were wanting? What about the times your anger made things worse, and ended up getting you less of what you were wanting? My guess is most of the time anger has not served you well, if you're honest with the scorecard. Certainly great anger doesn't tend to leave us closer to what we're really wanting.

The next time you feel anger you probably won't notice it until afterward. But once you realize you were recently angry, ask yourself a few simple questions:

- What did I care about?
- What outcome did I desire?
- Did my anger help me get it?
- What else might I have said or done?

If you're the type who never or seldom feels anger, you might not feel safe with that emotion (usually because of your childhood experiences), and so instead of anger you'll feel an intense sense of collapse or self-judgment, which is just anger facing inward—fuck *me* rather than fuck *you*. This tends to be on the parasympathetic side of the fight/flight/freeze response, but it operates the same way. Your unconscious choice, or reaction, is to move away from your care and into self-judgment and numbness as a way to not actually feel the care that had to arise first.

The realization and expression of care, instead of anger or collapse, can profoundly impact your life. Let's say your beloved does something that makes you genuinely upset, like forgets your birthday.

From a place of anger, you might say: "Jesus fucking Christ. What the fuck is wrong with you? Forget my fucking birthday? Could you be any more selfish or self-absorbed? It's literally the same day every year, and I don't ask for much. Just a little consideration!" This would very likely generate collapse or explosion from the person on the receiving end of this anger.

Conversely, if you were prone to collapse instead of anger, and your beloved forgot your birthday, you might respond not with an attack but with a neurotic accommodation. You might say: "You forgot?" A long silence. "I know you've been busy and have a lot on your mind. It's no problem.

We'll find another time to celebrate it." Yet inside, your heart is breaking and you're building up one of the great toxins of life: resentment. That resentment will get stored in your brain like in a bookkeeper's ledger, and after enough resentments are lodged in there, the relationship, over time, will start to profoundly suffer. Sex, intimacy, and a willingness for closeness will all start to collapse.

Neither anger nor collapse expresses any of the actual vulnerability that is under the reactive emotion. An integrated person might say: "Forgot my birthday? I must admit I feel like I'm not very important to you; like I don't matter very much. I know you're busy and I know this wasn't intentional, of course. I love you, but I feel afraid that you don't care as much about me as I thought. I'm wondering how we might make this right."

Feelings are information. When you get angry or you attack yourself or collapse, it means *you care about something*. It might also mean you feel vulnerable, overwhelmed, or scared as well. Anger covers that up so you don't have to feel the vulnerability—the care—that's driving it. If you feel the care when it arises, you can choose a response rather than reacting with anger or collapse.

When I met Junpo, I was in a very dynamic relationship that had me constantly fighting with my then-girlfriend. I once came to him, dismayed at how often and how badly I was getting triggered into explosive anger.

"You must care a great deal about her," he responded, "to be fighting that much." This completely floored me—it was immediately obvious and immediately deeply confusing. "Is the anger working?" he then asked. I admitted it wasn't working. "Maybe you should try something different," he suggested.

If you can feel the caring and the vulnerability, what arises instead of anger is something much more powerful: clarity. Clarity, unlike anger, keeps a channel open to the heart and to the cortex, which means you're in touch with your care and with the fact that a boundary may need defending. You gain the power of anger—focus, intensity, single-mindedness. But you lose the downsides—emotional blindness, impulsivity, unskillful defense, prefrontal cortex shutdown. You gain everything and lose nothing, because you get to *choose* your response to your care rather than have it chosen for you.

Trained fighters, no matter if they're MMA or Navy Seals, know how to respond to the impulse of anger in a high-stakes fight. They respond by finding the clarity instead of the anger, which enables them to fight back using all of their brains and bodies. Yet those same highly trained fighters may struggle to apply that exact same principle inside of their marriage, their community, their politics, or their family. The gift of anger, which is deep clarity, is lost.

THE TRUTH OF FEAR

We can experience fear in many ways in life. We might be afraid of public speaking, or afraid of becoming a parent. Flying or turbulence might scare us, or leaving our job to do what our heart most desires. We might be afraid of getting trapped in a relationship, being alone in life, or not realizing our full potential. Maybe marriage scares us senseless, or monogamy. Or open relationships. Or heights. Fear can come to us in a thousand ways, big and small, yet its message is always the same: *You're not safe, so stop and listen to me.*

If anger is fueled by care and vulnerability, what is it that fuels fear? The best example I can give of the truth of fear is from the author and meditation instructor Andrew Holecek, who has written extensively on Tibetan Dream Yoga. I was at a conference where he was a speaker, and after his talk he opened the floor for questions. A young woman stood up and was handed a microphone, the more than 150 people there all waiting for her question.

"Oh my god," she said breathlessly, voice noticeably shaking, "I'm *so* nervous!"

Holecek smiled, "So hang on. Take a moment to feel that energy in your body."

"It's intense!" she said, to some laughter.

"Yes! Just feel it. Feel it fully for a moment."

She did. I could see her clearly and could see the slight tremble in her body even from twenty feet away.

"Feel how fully *alive* you are, how much life force is running through you!"

She did and her whole body softened. She nodded, and when she spoke again her voice was steady. I no longer remember her question, but I do remember Holecek's wisdom. This kind of fear, like anger at the state of the environment or the guy in the White House, is a secondary emotion. It never arises on its own, but only in response to a deeper, truer feeling that drives it into existence.

In most circumstances, like with the young woman, what's under our fear is *excitement*. It might be the excitement of a speeding train coming toward us as a teenager on a train track. It could be the excitement of speaking publicly, or changing our career, or asking someone we love to marry us, or bungee jumping off a bridge. *Excitement* and *opportunity* will often cause fear to arise in response to those deeper, truer feelings. Junpo used to tell us that *fear is opportunity in disguise.*

As with anger, the next time you feel fear arise, you can run through a few simple questions (if not in the moment, then as soon as you realize that it paralyzed you):

- Was there excitement there?
- What might be possible if I look at this as an opportunity?
- What might I gain?
- Why might this scare me?

For instance, you might notice someday that you really want to step away from your day job and start your own business, but you're afraid of taking the first step because you fear being poor and running out of money. You might want to listen to the wisdom of the fear and leave wisely and with a good plan, but you'll never leave if you can't uncover the powerful coil of excitement and opportunity to bring your gifts more fully into the world. The fear is keeping you safe, which isn't a bad thing. But it's hard to spread your wings and fly if you're afraid of falling.

THE CHOICE INSIDE OF ANGER AND FEAR

Junpo taught that no one has ever made us angry or caused us to collapse. Not once. You have always chosen that, consciously or unconsciously, every time. Anger and turning away are our choices, and when we're willing to take radical responsibility for those actions we stop being victims and instead become *the creators of our own lives*, fully in control of life as it is in this moment.

Your boss can't make you angry, nor can your kids, your spouse, the "other" political party, the nature of the world, or your childhood. The person in the White House has never made you angry—nor has the jerk who cuts you off in traffic. Your abusive father didn't make you angry, nor your narcissistic boyfriend. The patriarchy can't make you angry, nor can people who are "too woke." No one has ever shamed you or caused you to turn away, either. You can't be shamed. You can't be made angry. You can't be made to collapse. Only you can overdo this, only you and only you alone, again and again and again, forever putting the blame in the wrong place: outside of yourself. You react unconsciously rather than choose your response, wisely and compassionately. For all of this there is a choice point—*your* choice point—even if you can't see it.

Most of the time it seems like we just fly into a reaction. Meditation offers a deeper way for us to uncover choice and have more impact on ourselves than psychotherapy alone can offer. Junpo, for instance, had a huge advantage in spending six years in a monastery, where he learned to quiet his mind. In the stillness he allowed there, he was able to witness the moment when he would get triggered. Rather than "flying into a rage" or becoming a victim to his own reactivity, he'd notice that a trigger had fired inside of his mind. Awareness would watch it happen. As I already discussed, Zen training then teaches you how to remain unreactive to the trigger. You wait until the trigger has passed, bypassing it until you can back into life without reactivity. Zen teaches you that this is the goal—to bypass.

This is better than reacting, and we'd be lucky if most of the world did this. But as Junpo realized after he became a roshi, there's no wisdom, no self-understanding, and no healing without choosing to turn directly into the trigger and to face it, head-on. Instead of letting it arise and fall away, we can notice it arise and then choose to turn completely into it.

First, let's understand better what happens when we get triggered—and from a spiritual perspective rather than a psychological one. First we need to go back to our definitions around consciousness and awareness.

Consciousness, you'll recall, is the entire self-system of the ego, the unconsciousness, and the self-awareness of all the components of the self. Our *consciousness* can be expanded or small, spiritual or profane, and it strongly colors how we experience the endless and undifferentiated flow of reality which, to remind you, doesn't much care what you think or feel about it—it just goes on being real.

Awareness comes before consciousness. Without awareness there is nowhere for consciousness to arise. This might just sound like a bunch of hot air unless you've experienced it, and I won't waste time or energy trying to convince you. Hopefully some of the practices at the end of this book can help to give you that experience for yourself. For now, let's just presume that I'm telling the truth, and that awareness is aware and that it is always here, at the root of your consciousness. If that is true, then it would follow that getting triggered would look something like this:

REACTIVITY	CHOOSE YOUR RESPONSE
1. Awareness is aware	1. Awareness is aware
2. Awareness sees or hears something	2. Awareness sees or hears something
3. Consciousness begins processing it	→ **There is Noticing**
4. An impact occurs inside the brain and the body (adrenaline, cortisol)	3. Consciousness begins processing it
5. A feeling arises (care, fear)	→ **You Notice**
6. A reaction happens (trigger reaction, like anger or collapse)	4. An impact occurs inside the brain and the body (adrenaline, cortisol)
→ **You Notice**	→ **You Notice**
7. **Your reaction prevents you from noticing that care, vulnerability, and/or fear were present.**	5. A feeling arises (care, fear)
	→ **You Turn Into the Feeling**
	6. **You choose to respond with clarity, curiosity, and healthy boundaries around the truth of your feelings.**

Notice there is no stopping the triggered response. But with meditation practice, you can learn and experience that there is more space between sensing something and our reaction to it than you can imagine. It's only microseconds between a stimulus and a reaction. Yet to someone who has a meditative mind, microseconds can literally pass like minutes. In the concentration meditation offered in Zen, you can do much more than simply witness your emotions arising. You can *turn into them*, follow them down to what is *really* going on. And then everything that arises is a wonderful teacher: Jealousy, anger, shame, lust, and envy (just to name a few emotions) can awaken you rather than be something in the way of your precious spiritual self.

AN UNENLIGHTENED VIEW OF EMOTIONS

For most of us, the arising of feelings goes something like this:

Stimulus
- → consciousness
- → habitual memory/conditioning
- → habitual reaction
- → no information is received
- → conditioned behavior continues
- → aversion to a deeper truth

EXAMPLE:

Stimulus: *someone cuts you off in traffic*
- → consciousness *notices*
- → habitual memory/conditioning: *you slam on the brakes and a deeply unconscious memory of your father's road rage gets triggered*
- → habitual reaction: *you "fly into a rage"*
- → no information is received
- → conditioned behavior continues
- → aversion to a deeper truth

You can hear this unconscious view of our emotions reflected in our language when it sounds like this:

"I just flew into a rage"

"She made me angry."

"When I see the president, I just go red with anger."

"How dare those people to try and take away my rights!" (Conservatives with the right to guns, or liberals with the right to choose.)

There is no room to *choose* a response. You simply *react* in a way similar to the conditioned and predictable behavior that we see all the time on social media. If we're honest, this is most of us most of the time: Conditioned creatures who react to stimuli in predictable ways.

AN ENLIGHTENED VIEW OF EMOTIONS

The bypassing that Junpo was taught in Zen works something like this:

Awareness
- → stimulus
- → consciousness
- → habitual memory/conditioning
- → **"listen"**
- → conditioned behavior stopped
- → no information is received
- → no reaction

Look at what's different here: For one, the traditional meditation student is aware of awareness, which is to say they can access the truth of their witnessing mind which is the first to purely notice that something has happened. *They notice that they noticed*, and then there's the same arc as for the unenlightened person: *stimulus, consciousness, habitual memory and conditioning*. But then the traditional meditator will "listen" to their reactive mind and their desire to *do something* in response to the stimuli. Instead of simply reacting, they will instead focus on their reactive mind, arising and falling away, and choose not to act. Yet they will not receive any information in their feeling. This person might express emotions like this:

UNENLIGHTENED VIEW	ENLIGHTENED VIEW
"I just flew into a rage."	"I felt some energy arising a moment ago."
"She made me angry."	"I simply avoid that woman."
"When I see the president, I just go red with anger."	"When I see the president, I see the violence of duality perfectly manifested."
"How dare those people to try and take away my rights!"	"When they fight to take away my rights, it's because they don't understand the nature of conflict."

The conditioned response is interrupted. One rests in awareness until the contraction subsides. The emotionality is bypassed. In traditional meditation, feelings are something that are to be seen and largely ignored, the same as with any stimulus that arises and falls away.

AN INTEGRATED VIEW OF EMOTIONS

When we combine the insights of meditation with those of modern psychotherapy, we can finally find a bridge to cross—one that does not simply bypass feelings, but one that is in touch with the truth. Those feelings and that conditioning are, in fact, impermanent, yet they are hugely influential (often in hugely negative ways) in our lives.

The integrated practitioner uses this to have a discerning relationship with feeling that looks something like this:

Awareness
- → stimulus
- → consciousness
- → habitual memory/conditioning
- → "listen"
- → conditioned behavior stopped
- → **information is received**
- → **choose a conscious/different response**

Notice that this is similar to the process of a traditional meditator, but it changes with the last two steps. Rather than just waiting for the unpleasant reaction to pass, we turn into it fully, giving it our egoic attention. In other words, we ask: "What is this reaction really telling me?"

This approach could point to simple truths, such as that care underlies anger. It can also point to much larger truths, such as a deep childhood wound that has us unable to trust others in intimate relationships, or a strong sexual desire we don't understand that gets the better of us, or a need to dominate someone who challenges us. Fully understanding this—maybe with a skilled therapist who can help us delve into the shadows of our psyche—can help us determine what to keep inside the meditative space, and what to take out of it.

This person might express emotions like this:

UNENLIGHTENED VIEW	ENLIGHTENED VIEW	INTEGRATED VIEW
"I just flew into a rage."	"I felt some energy arising a moment ago."	"I'm upset because this is important to me."
"She made me angry."	"I simply avoid that woman."	"She did something that was unacceptable to me, and I had to draw a boundary."
"When I see the president, I just go red with anger."	"When I see the president, I see the violence of duality perfectly manifested."	"When I see the president, I have an almost irresistible urge to project my issues onto him because I see him destroying things I care about."
"How dare those people to try and take away my rights!"	"When they fight to take away my rights, it's because they don't understand the nature of conflict."	"When they fight to take away my rights, it's because the issue isn't being framed correctly to take into account their care and my care."

In the Integrated View, the truth of meditative mind is present, but so is the truth of vulnerability, care, and fear. This creates a radical difference in how we approach conflict and disharmony.

NO ONE HAS EVER MADE YOU ANGRY (REALLY)

In *The Heart of Zen,* Junpo walks us through a great example of how this can work in real life:

You might request that there be a change in behavior, so that a certain level of flirtation is agreed to be over the line. Some couples are comfortable with monogamy with no flirting. Some with lots of flirting. Some couples are polyamorous and have multiple sexual partners. What matters is getting the truth in the feeling and choosing your reaction from the depth of caring— while being honest about the fear and keeping a healthy boundary about what you are willing to tolerate and will not tolerate.

You get to choose. We never roll over and allow ourselves to become doormats. You may have to end a relationship because your beloved cannot honor your needs around monogamy, or polyamory. That will bring up a lot of fear and caring, for both people!

From a Zen perspective, there is nothing that can cause me to look away from any situation. Negative chosen reactivity causes violence expressed as jealousy, anger, shame, or disgust. True meditative awareness is boundless, limitless, imperturbable, and unshakable. The compassion found here knows no boundary, and this heart cannot be broken—only blown further open.

From this place, discriminating wisdom and right action flow as naturally as water down a hillside, you see.

Junpo was known to say many controversial things, designed to break the listener out of their habitual thinking and drive them into a place of *not knowing*. One of them was, "There are no victims in Zen." This was the kind of statement that immediately upset a good deal of the people in the room, and more than once a few would simply walk out after he said it, not waiting to see if there might be something to learn.

In the next chapter, I'll explore this controversial statement and see how it can be a key to the integration of your spiritual insight with emotional reality.

CHAPTER 6

Why There Are No Victims in Zen

Throughout this book I have maintained that, by their very definition, we cannot see our psychological shadows. If we can't see our shadows, how can we know where to look—and how can we hold others accountable for things that *they* might not be able to see? I once put this question to Junpo, who said, "Just look for the wake in your life—the places where you keep hurting others, hurting yourself, or keep coming up against the same problems."

An example might be that if you keep finding yourself in abusive or misattuned relationships. You can blame the patriarchy, blame the woman (or man, or human), blame your parents for how they screwed you up, or blame any other number of things outside of yourself. There may be some truth in that blaming, which I will get to shortly.

Yet it is also true that there is only one constant in your life, which is *you*. If you keep choosing bad partners, you may have shadow around intimacy. If you keep finding yourself running out of money and unable to play that game, you can blame capitalism or the system, and there may also be some truth in that blaming. And yet, just like with intimacy, no matter if your shadow was put there by your culture, your parents, your education, or anything else, it is ultimately your responsibility to understand it, disentangle yourself from it, and transcend that shadow. Here's how that work can be done.

When you look at your shadows in detail and discernment, you almost always find they contains "both/and" truths, not "either/or" ones. It may be true that you haven't stepped fully into your own power because of the patriarchy, and in that sense, it's not your fault. Yet it is your responsibly to empower yourself. Both/and are true. Being responsible for things that are not your fault does not mean you were not victimized, that there isn't something wrong or broken with the system, that you didn't suffer, or that radical change isn't needed. All it means is that you, and you alone, are ultimately responsible for your life and its circumstances as they are now.

Remember that the whole point of this book is that enlightenment includes all of reality as it is now, without our opinions or valuations of it. This is how you integrate this truth with the hard reality of victimization, shadow, ego story, and the messiness of being a human being.

Our shadows live in our seemingly unshakable long-standing patterns, like always being single, always choosing bad relationships, always losing our temper in certain situations, always being poor, always giving away too much of ourselves, or always standing apart and aloof from relationships. Maybe you are always seeking the perfect partner—"the one"—and so you're always disappointed in other people's inevitable humanness, or perhaps you always settle for someone less than what you deserve.

Remember what Junpo said, and what I already spent a good deal of time explaining in Chapter 3: You are a *process* and not a *self*, and that process is entirely conditioned. When you find pain points in your life, blaming the outside world will never help you move from being a victim to being a creator, from being conditioned to react instead of being able to choose a response. You can recondition yourself, change your process, so that like a factory that updates its machines, you can get a different output.

What I'm about to ask you to do will certainly trigger some readers, but nevertheless I would like you to trust me on this and follow through. Go slowly and let yourself feel your reaction:

- What does it feel like to take *full* responsibility for your life as it is, in this moment?
- What if *no one* and *no thing* was responsible for your life but you?
- What if it was also true that the stuck places in your life are, to this point, *not your fault*?
- Can you experience the feeling of full responsibility of your entire life, right now, without collapsing into anger or shame?

If you take full responsibility for your life, you may likely experience a great deal of fear, because your life is suddenly your own, without exception. If you recall from the previous chapter that fear is really just excitement, then what might you actually be excited about inside of all this freedom? Perhaps it's the terror of knowing that you have more control over your own life than you ever imagined possible, and that you have the power to recondition yourself in whatever way you can imagine. Yet your shadows often stand in the way of this process.

Once you see a shadow, the only way you can understand it and bring it to consciousness is to work with another human being, one who is able to reflect what *they're* seeing. I don't know of any times when someone has fully resolved a shadow by themselves, probably because we are wounded in relationship and therefore need to heal in relationship. This is normally done with a skilled therapist or coach, but any two people with reasonable observational skills can offer this to each other. Men and women's work —online or in-person coaching, mastermind groups, family constellations work, authentic relating, two friends sharing with the intention of seeing each other's blind spots, or any number of other modalities can help you to see your shadows, to see where your process is conditioned, and to begin the process of reconditioning those parts.

Junpo made the audacious statement that there are no victims in Zen. As a meditation master, part of his job was to shock people into listening more deeply than they ever had before, often by triggering an emotional response. In the victim-loving cultures of Boulder and the San Francisco Bay Area, this was an easy way for him to get a collective gasp from a crowd, and to set them up to want to argue with him about just how wrong, patronizing, and privileged he was. And they fell into an old Zen trick that, in the right hands, can end up opening people to seeing things a new way. For those who had the ears to hear it, Junpo's point was always a nuanced one, a point born out of his own severe abuse and a lifetime spent denying he was victimized, to then, reluctantly, realizing how deeply he'd been wounded, to finally working to set down that conditioning.

YOUR ANGST IS YOUR LIBERATION

Junpo was not denying that some people—even most people—are victimized at some point in their lives, or even throughout most of their lives. He was himself a survivor and saw firsthand how that shaped so much of him. He was all too aware of the push to blame victims, a push that was far more prevalent in his time than it is in ours.

It is vital that anyone who has experienced abuse and victimization recognize and come to terms with this. There is no bypassing allowing oneself to feel victimhood on the path to healing. For instance, if I leave my house this afternoon and am accosted by a group of men, beaten, and robbed, I could say a day later that I'm over the experience and I'm totally fine. Yet that would not be true. There would be deep physical and emotional impacts in my system that I would need to "own," or to acknowledge that were present. If I didn't *feel* the victimization, it would be impossible for me to *move past* being a victim. In order to heal, I would have to move through, not around, what happened to me. This is true for all humans, no matter if what happened to us was last week or sixty years in the past.

This isn't just about personal victimization but also cultural ones as well. We can look at the hot-button issues of race and gender all over the world. There are good arguments being made that women and people of color in the West have suffered a collective victimization at the hands of the dominant (white, straight, male) culture, experiencing everything from glass ceilings, to increased incarcerations and police shootings, to decreased access to advancement. Some of this victimization is very real (to what degree is open to debate and outside the scope of this book), but it must be acknowledged and felt before it can be metabolized and then most effectively addressed and changed.

If you don't allow yourself to feel your victimhood, you will have a compromised ability to take a stand, have healthy boundaries, and express healthy anger (which we've seen is actually deep clarity). This is vital for the expression and felt sense of healthy vulnerability and fear, which are necessary for you to feel if you're going to integrate your experience into something that leaves you more, not less, whole. That creates a person who is more empowered, not less. Who is more self-assured, not less. And who is more open-hearted and open-minded, not less.

If we don't first feel how we might have been victimized, we can't feel the depths of how much we've been negatively impacted by it. *We can't heal things that we can't see.*

Part of what happens when we're victimized by a human or a culture (as opposed to an earthquake or car accident or near-drowning) is we internalize the voices that have told us we're a mess, or not enough, or weak, or dangerous, or lazy, or deserving of abuse or a lack of respect, or a second-class citizen. The standard defense against rape for years, for instance, amounted to, "Well, what was she wearing?" This is a classic example of blaming the victim, and many victims of sexual abuse presumed they were somehow at fault in some way, big or small. They were not. Those external voices of blame can become internal ones, and those voices end up subjugating ourselves in one of the more pernicious effects of victimization.

Victims of sexual abuse sometimes wonder what they did to "deserve" it. Victims of cultural abuse may tell themselves how stupid and unworthy they are of success. Victims of emotional abuse may tell themselves how unworthy of love they really are, how messed up and deserving of the mess of their life.

At some point in the process of moving into fully feeling how much we've been victimized, it can be helpful to say the words, "What happened to me was wrong. And it wasn't my fault." That's truly being a victim—you did nothing to deserve what happened to you, and it may continue to limit you, but these things are not your fault.

If you're Black, it's not your fault you were profiled. If you're a woman, it's not your fault you were denied a raise that went to a less qualified, male coworker. If you're a survivor of childhood abuse, it's not your fault you were abused, and it's not your fault you may have trouble trusting people in intimate partnership. If your partner hits you, you did nothing to deserve that physical violence.

The word "survivor" can be a helpful one, so long as it's held lightly and in a nuanced way. Identifying as a survivor and not a victim can allow for growth and change rather than stagnation and calcification, and sometimes we can even grow past the need to use even that word.

The vital first step is to be willing, when you're ready, to move past your feeling of victimhood. As any decent therapist knows, it's unwise to simply stop your story with the full acceptance of being a victim. To be free of victimhood one must, at some point, choose to move out of it. This does not mean that you weren't the victim of that act, crime, or cultural violation—only that you're choosing to no longer let that identity be fixed there.

You might think of it like this: If you were working with a therapist or coach trying to find traction in your life and they kept you in the role of a victim, excusing your failures as the full fault and full responsibility of society, you could never actualize your human potential. You would be stuck, waiting for something outside of yourself to take control of your life.

What's needed is something that can help you to acknowledge the realness of your victimhood while also allowing you to move past it to reclaim your life on your own terms. This "transcend and include" model is part of what Junpo was, provocatively, pointing to when he said there are no victims in Zen.

There's one more dynamic worth mentioning here, which is something known as the Drama Triangle.[27] It holds that a dynamic can be created that keeps us stuck in the victim mindset by creating two other types of categories: the persecutor and the rescuer. The role of the victim is to be fully

---

27 David Emerald, *The Power of TED**, 3rd ed. (Edinburgh: Polaris Publishing, 2016).

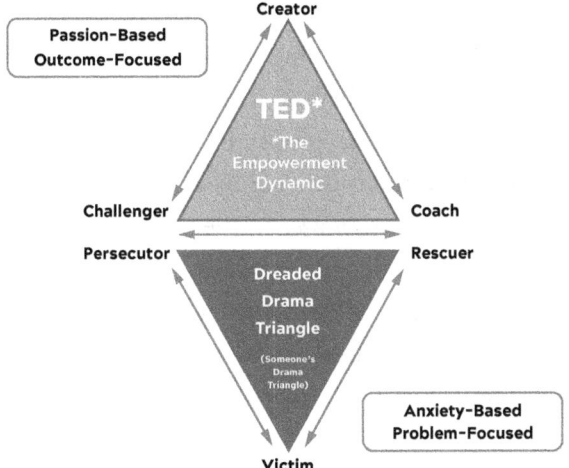

identified with their lack of power. They, and the rescuer, perceive all of the real power to lie with the persecutor. It is therefore the rescuer's job to "save" the victim and to denigrate the persecutor, but the rescuer's motivation is primarily selfish—to make themselves feel better about the victim's status. We see this, of course, in immature identity politics, which can be deeply insulting to the intelligence, drive, and self-awareness of affected victims of social or cultural oppression.[28]

---

28 The University of Nevada, Las Vegas issued an apology because it sent out an email to new students with advice on how to lower the risk of assault—things such as not speaking on your phone, being aware of your physical surroundings, and walking confidently. The school, after receiving blowback and the letter below, chose to retract the advice and offer a full apology. This makes as much sense of offering an apology for telling people how to prepare for a hurricane because that might somehow shame hurricane survivors. The actual letter from a campus victim rights group read as follows:

"For folks who've been impacted directly or indirectly by violence, it may have been frustrating or even painful to open up your email and read the same harmful and victim-blaming language. The CARE Center and SDSJ recognize that framing violence prevention around "being confident," "being alert and aware of your surroundings" and other tips that place responsibility on the individual to avoid being attacked erase the lived experiences of so many of us. We want to reiterate that no matter the circumstances, victim-survivors are not responsible for crimes or violence committed against them. Our hope and commitment for the future is that you never are made to feel like violence was your fault, and instead that you feel cared for and supported by the institution you've entrusted with your safety and education."

I made the point that victimhood is best understood in a both/and model, one that includes transcending and including the complex truth of victimization so you can move beyond it and back into empowerment. It is in that vein that the Drama Triangle can be transcended and include more active and whole roles without denying what happened. The three archetypes of *victim*, *rescuer*, and *perpetrator* can be transcended into *creator*, *coach*, and *challenger*.

The victim is no longer stuck in their role of needing to be rescued. Likewise, persecutors and rescuers are not stuck in static roles but allowed to be in dynamic and fluid process as well. This doesn't negate the reality of what we might find in the world but it does put the focus on movement.

As already mentioned, a coach or therapist cannot help a client if they are only willing to see that person as a victim. At some point, they will work to help that person reclaim their autonomy and use their experience to become a creator of a new reality that sees what happened to them but is no longer bound by or defined solely by it. In that example, the coach or therapist is acting as coach, not a rescuer, and slowly shifting the sense of a static perpetration into a sense of challenge to be overcome. Movements like Restorative Justice are also designed to break this chain of victim-persecutor-rescuer, and allow all three to grow into a more healing and empowered creator-challenger-coach dynamic.

Junpo Roshi:

> *Awakening starts with a deep curiosity, a deep questioning of who you really are. Then you must have the experience of turiyatita, or oneness, for yourself.*
>
> *Then, based on your experience, not theory or ideas, for the first time you have a choice. To live in freedom, or to continue to live in reactive patterns, bound to your ego's whims and conditioning; a dog trained by your parents and your culture and your genes. Sit. Stay. Beg. Complain. Achieve. Run. You must remember that you are actually choosing your habitual reactions. No one has made you react in a certain way; no one has ever made you*

WHY THERE ARE NO VICTIMS IN ZEN

angry, shamed you, or caused you to numb out. All the dumb shit you do is not caused by anyone else but you; not mom and dad's fault, not because you've been culturally repressed, not because of anything external.

There are no victims in Zen.

I never said the truth was easy. Emotional koans can solve the problem of our ignorant choices and victimhood, and transform them into conscious responses and real, lived empowerment. Not from the ego, but through the ego.

When Junpo and I were working on *A Heart Blown Open*, we met for coffee in my hometown of Boulder. From the moment I saw him, I could tell he was upset. We got our coffees and sat down.

"What's up, Junpo?" I asked.

He shook his head. "Ellen," he said. Ellen was one of Junpo's attendants and a masterful cook who had been living with him from time to time, preparing food, acting as a bookkeeper, and helping to manage his day-to-day business. She and I were good friends.

"What about her?"

He shook his head. Tears came to the edges of his eyes. "I was looking over my income statements, and I saw there were a bunch of charges on my credit card to Apple Music, which I don't use. And I knew. I knew right away."

I had no idea what that meant. "You knew…?"

"She was embezzling from me. When I looked into the books, about sixty-thousand over the last two years."

"Holy shit!" Ellen was a great and kind woman who had shared more than one meal and whisky with me over the years.

"What are you going to do?"

"Well, everyone thinks I should call the cops on her and prosecute her."

"Are you?"

"Absolutely fucking not." He looked at me very intensely. "I told her she needs to repay me, and can do it over the next two or three years. Monthly payments. And then we'll see if she wants to come back into the community."

"Jesus," I said. "That's a pretty big betrayal."

He signed. "Yeah. Well, I just keep asking myself: What did I do to give her the impression that this kind of behavior would be acceptable with me?"

I was shocked. His takeaway wasn't about her at all. It wasn't how could she have done this to him, or how could she have been so selfish. It also wasn't a collapsed version of the same thing—how could he have been so stupid or blind to hire her? Rather, it was a radical ownership of their relationship, and an honest inquiry for him about how he might have made a mistake in his orientation to her as a teacher and a friend. *I just keep asking myself: What did I do to give her the impression that this kind of behavior would be acceptable with me?*

Let me give one more example of why there are no victims in Zen, this time from my personal experience. As I've mentioned already, I had an at-times traumatic childhood involving enmeshment and 1970s-style "tough love" parenting, an utter lack of emotional attunement from my mother compounded by our enmeshment,[29] layered on top of a middle-class upbringing, a good education, and a loving but emotionally-distant father. It's a complicated past, as are most of ours. The experiences of my childhood and teen years, however, were traumatic enough to have an impact on my ability to be in a stable and long-term relationship, to be able to experience emotions without them overpowering me, and to be willing to show vulnerability to others, among other ways the victimization I experienced manifested in my adult years, making me a victim of my experiences, at least at first.

---

29 Enmeshment is when a child and a parent's emotions are "enmeshed" so that when the parent gets upset, the child feels it and vice-versa. The parent is unable to separate her/his emotional reality from the separate emotional reality of the child. The child then feels they must caretake their parent's emotional distress and behave in ways that will minimize how they feel so as to not upset the parent. In my relationship to my mother as a child, I became "hyper-attuned" to her emotional state so as not to upset her.

Attunement is simply being able to "attune" to the emotions of another person. This can be done with healthy boundaries, say in therapy. But in an enmeshed relationship, a parent is unable to attune to the child and the child must attune to the parent. This can create life-long challenges in healthy boundaries in intimate relationships.

WHY THERE ARE NO VICTIMS IN ZEN

My relationship to it evolved like this:

1. **Survival Mode:** I'm not fucked up. You are. (When I was living at home and acting out by drinking, getting arrested, and challenging any kind of authority figure.)
2. **Victim:** I'm a total fuckup and unworthy of love. I'm lucky to have found anyone who is willing to love me at all. (Moving out of my childhood home but then internalizing the external voices of my childhood. I was now, unconsciously, my own oppressor.)
3. **Perpetrator:** My mother and my teachers fucked me up and it's their fault. (When I began therapy and started seeing patterns that were put into me from my childhood. I now saw my mother and my Catholic upbringing as my oppressors and me as their victim. Many people were very happy to try and rescue me from this by commiserating with my story.)
4. **Rescuer:** My mother and educators fucked me up. It's their fault but I can free myself from what they did to me (Trying to rescue that part of myself that was a victim. In other words, I moved from needing an external rescuer to rescue my victim, to having an internal rescuer—a further step toward empowerment and ownership.)
5. **Creator:** My mother and educators conditioned me in the way they were conditioned, but I can recondition myself. (Realizing that trauma gets passed down generation to generation. The Drama Triangle is broken because I can now see my mother and educators as Challengers who helped me grow, not as Perpetrators who forced me into victimhood.)
6. **Full Empowerment:** It's no one's fault but it is my responsibility. (The cycle is fully transformed. No one is at fault. Those who conditioned me were themselves conditioned. It is entirely on me to live with the life circumstances handed to me exactly as they are. There is no one to blame anymore—not her, not them, not me, not working-class Irish culture, not anything else. There are just my childhood challenges that allowed me to transform into the man I am today).

This was my own radical responsibility on the way to letting go of my victimhood without denying victimization happened. This does not mean that the impacts of my childhood are not with me. They will forever be a part of me, voices and energetic patterns inside that I must always be working with, and on. Junpo's point was that we all have a choice to take ourselves through a process like this, no matter what our past looks like and no matter what forces seem aligned against us.

One of the ways we can work through these issues in our own life is through emotional koans.

EMOTIONAL KOANS

In Zen, a traditional koan is a question given that cannot be answered with your rational mind. The answer must come from a deeper place of insight, of having an experience of being bigger than the question. Koan study isn't the study of metaphysics of philosophy, like a well-trained, Oxford-educated debater. When a Zen master says something like, "you can transcend good and evil entirely," or that Zen is "beyond all morality," those are not philosophical statements to be debated and analyzed. They are statements of insight that need to be realized, in one's being and not just in one's mind. In the mind they produce either paradox or highly unethical behavior, because the wisdom invited by the koan transcends what thinking ever understands on its own.

Koans are about an experience beyond ego, beyond story, and beyond concepts, identity, or control of reality. Zen is indeed beyond good and evil and beyond morality, but that truth, that experience, will bring you to your knees and have your heart break open with compassion and love for all sentient beings. Behaving selfishly will be inconceivable when you realize the insight of that koan. It brings you to your knees not because you're free of morality, but because you see beyond the stories of morality and, more so, see into the fire of your own blazing heart, where acting selfishly is as inconceivable as cutting out your own tongue. You are beyond good and evil, which doesn't mean you're an amoral asshole. But you might not seem very moral by the compass of your peers, or your culture. Traditional koans are used to help a student deepen their insight around the relative inside of the absolute, the absolute inside of the relative, and the integration of these so they can be dissolved entirely.

Emotional koans work a similar way. These are Junpo's unique contributions to Zen. In traditional Zen, you'll recall, emotions are things to be bypassed. But in Junpo's Mondo Zen, they're designed to allow us to get the *information in the feeling* so it can be integrated. With an emotional koan, we find a place where we know we will get hooked, or triggered, in the future. We then allow that this is a place where we could find liberation from our egoic self. How? Well, remember that from an integrated spirituality, emotional triggers operate like this:

Awareness → stimulus → consciousness → habitual memory/conditioning → "listen" → conditioned behavior stopped → information is received → choose a conscious/different response

When you first notice that you're having a habitual reaction, "listen" to it, stop the habitual reaction, get the information in the feeling, and choose a different response. This allows you to be emotionally mature, and this alone can transform your life. This is one way that your angst can be your liberation, and this was the entire focus of Chapter 5.

Yet there is a deeper practice as well, one that will help you to experience awareness as awareness. If you know that a situation gets you hooked or triggered, the next time it happens you can use it to awaken, in a very literal way. You have to be willing to pay attention deeply, and to notice when awareness first sees that thing that upsets you. It could be a car cutting you off, or your partner raising their voice in a particular way, or a phone call from your mother, or news you read about a certain topic that just gets your blood boiling. If you know where you're going to get triggered, you can practice paying attention the next time you know it will happen. Then, you can see for yourself that awareness is always aware *before* "you" get triggered.

Awareness comes before "I." Just like awareness hears sound before your consciousness valuates it as good or bad or "a bell" or "a kid crying," so too awareness sees the event that will causes you to get triggered. It is literally

Buddha-mind, or awakening itself, or the mind of God, that sees this, and *you can experience that every time you get triggered.*

Junpo often said, "Your angst is your liberation." That is precisely what he meant. This is why liberation is so close at hand that almost none of us can actually see it. It's so obvious, and so close to you, that it's very easy to miss because you believe your mind moves fast, when in fact your mind only moves fast if you're solely identified with your consciousness.

When you "listen" to that habitual trigger—your conditioned response— it reminds you that you've been aware the whole time. With practice, this shocks your consciousness into shutting up for a few moments to allow *awareness of awareness* to flow through you. Your identity then gets increasingly rooted in awareness and less and less rooted in your consciousness. Triggering events become be the fuel that allow you to push deeper and deeper into awareness.

Our emotions are information, although most of us ignore the information and instead create shit stories about our world or about ourselves. Liberation comes when you are willing to get the information in the emotions by dropping into awareness. This allows you to see through, deconstruct, and reinform your sense of self to include the fact that the self is entirely an illusion, a construct of the ego.

Our thoughts, stories, and identities are not permanent and will not last. We are a process and not a self, remember. Your ego may experience the terror of this realization of the self not being real and of your stories of the world being mostly constructs more than true reflections of what is. My ego has certainly experienced this terror. But you can let go of this terror by continuing to turn into it, deepening your spiritual insight by grounding your identity in awareness itself, releasing your attachment to your stories, getting the information in your feelings, and changing your understanding of what and who you are.

This coming week, you will inevitably find yourself triggered by something in life. It's predictable, and there's an invitation to know yourself well enough to know when this will likely be. This is your emotional koan.

WHY THERE ARE NO VICTIMS IN ZEN

It could be mild, like boredom during a weekly work Zoom call. It could be more intense, like road rage coming home at the end of a long day. It could be deeply ingrained and old, like the feeling of having to call a parent over the weekend to prevent them from getting upset. It might be depression that doesn't seem to have a cause, or anxiety at the thought of getting up for an early morning meeting. It could also seem righteous, like the anger at reading something in the news involving the "other" political party, or the state of the environment, or the current state of LGBTQ rights. It doesn't really matter. If you know it's coming, you can use it as a place to do something aside from react, like a well-trained Pavlovian dog drooling at the sound of the bell. You can use it to awaken, first emotionally and then into a place of liberation from reactivity itself.

You are not a victim. Or a creator. You are not a rescuer. Or a coach. And you are not a perpetrator, or a challenger. You are none of these things. You are before Abraham. You are the Alpha and the Omega, both. You are timeless and deathless, have no boundary, cannot be born and cannot die. You and God are not two, nor are you and the thing you hate the most in life. You are not of this world and yet you are in every part of it, every molecule, every grain of sand. And every time you get triggered by your story, you have a chance to realize this for yourself. Only you have this power. No teacher does, and no teaching. You and you alone can experience depth beyond anything you thought was possible, to be liberated of any construct whatsoever. To be unbreakable, unflappable, full of compassion and love and insight, and utterly beyond ideas of right or wrong.

But you may need to practice as if your life depends on it.

CHAPTER 7

Can You Choose Enlightenment?

The word "enlightenment" is problematic because it implies a permanent state, an arrival ground more like "graduated" than the experience of an ongoing awakened state of being. *Sustained enlightening* is a better and more accurate description because it reflects the importance of ongoing mindfulness and choice in the life of any awakened being. As Junpo warned me early in our training together, we must be very careful with the language we use because it can inadvertently trap us. For instance, for the first two or so years I was training with him, he would often refer to awakening in some version of this:

When you find yourself in an awakened state, you'll find that everything there has an element of perfection to it.

He realized that the language itself was incongruent with his own experience; awakening wasn't and could never be "there," and so he changed his language to talk about enlightenment being "here."

When you find yourself in an awakened state, you'll find that everything here has an element of perfection to it.

That one-word change, from "there" to "here," is an indication of how and where we choose to awaken. We don't choose at dinner tonight, or after our upcoming retreat, or when we've had a good night's sleep, or once we get that job we really want. The choice is now, here, which is where we'll find awakening.

Let's dive into the nature of this choosing, of the power we hold to awaken ourselves into the fullness of this moment.

KNOW WHO'S CHOOSING

This question gets to the heart of your spiritual seeking. As you've seen repeatedly, you are not your thoughts, ideas, stories, personas, projections, opinions, or views of the world. All of those things arise in time, change over time, and will end in time. Which raises an interesting question: If you remove all of those things, then who are you? Who is it who would choose to awaken? Does Keith, the author of this book, choose his awakening like he chooses curly fries at the local drive-in?

Yes and no. Let me answer that question more completely with a question of my own. Can you, reader, tell me who you are without telling me what you *think* or what you *feel*? Who are you that is beyond thinking and feeling, or concepts or beliefs?

Who are you?

We're not sitting face to face, and so I can't play this Q and A with you. That's unfortunate, because having this realization can cause a radical shift in how you view the world and yourself. So I would ask you to slow down here as you're reading. Take your time and give yourself some space to feel into how you might answer, into what might be true for you.

Not long after meeting Junpo, sometime in early 2008, we sat down together, face to face, and he asked me that very question.

"Who are you? Tell me without telling me what you think or feel."

I considered. I knew I couldn't say "man" or "American" or "writer," or anything like that, because those identities can be easily deconstructed. Since you weren't always a man or a writer, and since you won't be an American after you die, those impermanent identities are just that—impermanent. When a Zen master asks you who you are, they want to know who you are before thought, before feeling, before a story of you of any kind. After all, you can sit there with no thoughts in your head, and you're still sitting there without anything to define you to yourself. So who are you, really, below the level of identity?

I was new to Boulder at the time, but I was a fast study. Boulder had a lot of "self-love" and "love is all" kind of yoga and spiritual circles, so I took a shot.

"Love," I said to Junpo, feeling like that wasn't a bad answer. He laughed. "You told me what you thought," he observed.

"Yeah, true enough."

"*And* you weren't very convincing," he added.

I laughed. "Awareness," I said. This time I flattened my tone to sound more confident. He nodded. "You told me what you thought again," he remarked. "And besides, *you're* not awareness any more than *you're* love."

I gave him a questioning look.

"Love is love, baba," he said. ("Baba" was a term of endearment he often called his students.) "Awareness is aware. God is aware. Love is aware. God is love." He shook his head. "I don't see *you* in there *anywhere*." He smiled. "You're still talking with your head." He jabbed a finger into his own temple.

"Okay," I said, trying to not think at all. "Emptiness," I breathed, very Zen-like. He just shook his head. I felt into my heart, felt into my body. "Presence," I offered.

"You told me what you feel. Good, but feelings come and go, just like thoughts. Go deeper, baba. Deeper." He held me with the intensity of his blue eyes.

How would you answer him? As you look into yourself, from your ego, who are you? Can you find anything that was there before you were born and will survive death? Something that comes before any self-referential thought or self-oriented feeling?

I knew, sitting with Junpo, that I wasn't love or awareness or emptiness or presence. I knew he'd bat down any temporal identity, like *writer* or *man* or *American*, as thoughts and constructs. And so we sat and looked at one another. He waited. And he waited some more. Minutes passed. Many of them, my mind furiously working, relaxing, seeking, surrendering, but nowhere could I find an answer that would satisfy him. I didn't fucking know, I realized. I didn't know who I was, and I had no way to answer him. Whatever Zen game this was, I either had been beaten or wasn't clever enough to play, and I was about to say as much to Junpo.

And then it hit me: *I didn't know who I was.*

I didn't know who I was.

As I sat there looking within myself, there was only a black hole of mystery. I wasn't anything that I could think or feel, and yet I was. How was that possible? Who was looking, who was realizing this? "Keith" was just a temporal construct, conditioned and constructed like so many Legos made into a man-shaped toy.

This truth, this terrifying truth, was that I didn't know. "I don't know," I finally whispered, unable to hold back the tears. All my life, thirty-some odd some years at that point, and I'd never come close to seeing it. *I didn't know who the fuck I was*, and I had been stuffing personas and relationships and ambition and stories and opinions and judgments and a false self-assuredness into that hole the entire time. My breath hitched and caught and I lifted a hand to cover my face, feeling the shame of tears on my cheeks (an old story of mine, since let go, that shame arose anytime tears would come).

Terror, cold and tense, slid up my spine and coiled around my heart. How could I not know? How was that possible? I had a vocation, a passion for writing, was divorced, was intelligent, was a marital artist, was a child of my parents, was an American, was a lover of Integral theory… *I am so many things, so many identities, and none of them are real!*

What sort of Zen trickery was this?

"You've been running from this a long time," Junpo said, almost inaudibly. "Take a moment to let it in. I won't leave you here." His eyes steeled. "*I will not turn away.*"

More tears, for his words hit something deep inside of me, some then-unseen wound of childhood. To have a man, this man, witness me in this collapsing, fear-filled state, and to have him so leaned into me, so fully present, so completely there, was truly unlike anything I'd ever experienced. I'd always suffered alone, cried alone, struggled alone. (It would take another twelve or thirteen years to fully unwind that conditioning, a story I'll leave for the Postscript in this book.)

Only because of him was I able to lean into the cold tendrils of terror that were screaming at me to stop doing this, shut it down, stand up, and go do something that felt life-affirming, like fucking or drinking or riding my motorcycle far too fast. I needed to convince myself that I was real. I didn't want to sit there with him, to sit inside of the horror of the realization that there was no self, there was no me, that I was as impermanent as a cloud in a summer sky. I looked deeply, desperately, into Junpo's eyes, and he held me there with his kindness and with his intense and hard-earned wisdom. And he did not turn away, not for one second.

I don't know who I am. What a powerful insight! What a powerful truth to feel in the depth of your being. Once I admitted that truth I could begin my spiritual training in earnest, because I'd given up my ideas about what the world was and was not. I'd emptied my cup of opinions and firmly held beliefs about how the world "was" so it could be filled with a new kind of insight, a new kind of tea that wasn't about what I liked and didn't, what I thought was just and unjust, what I knew to be right and wrong.

In places like Boulder and the Bay Area, when I ask students this question they will almost always answer, "Love." And I ask, "Are you love all the time, in all places and all situations? Have you always acted from this love, been this love, and never once done something not from love?"

"Well, no…" they'll admit.

"So you're not love," I will say. "Love arises within you. Sometimes you are love, and sometimes you are not. But you aren't something that comes and goes." The ego needs its personas, and *love as identity* (as opposed to love as experience) is one of the hardest ones to let go, because it's just so damn spiritual. If you found yourself saying *love* when asked this question, you might look more deeply to see how true it really is for you. Because *love* sounds good, but I've only met a handful of Christian monks who could tell me that and fully mean it, because they meant love without ego, love without attachment, love without story, love without morality, and love without boundaries of any kind whatsoever. That kind of love is as rare as the most precious of gems, and even those of us with children and vast experiences of human love have never touched even a corner of this kind of luminous, transcendent love.

Anything you use to define yourself can be shown to be transient. At some point in time, it didn't exist, and now it does, and at some point in time it will no longer exist. When you admit that you don't know who you are, you get a sense of why it's so important to stuff various identities into that hole, because not knowing who you are, from an ego perspective, is terrifying. The terror of there actually being no self is true terror indeed. On the other side, however, that terror is liberation from a false self that is the prison you've come to know and to love.

I invite you to say the words, now, and to really say them as if they might be true and, perhaps, even truer than anything you've yet said in your life.

"I don't know who I am."

The world may be suddenly transformed from something you think you understand and control, to something that is endlessly creative and utterly out of your control, and out of your ability to understand and categorize. Facing that potential terror of admitting you don't know who you are is the first step toward the wisdom of embracing what that truth can show you. This is an important step in how we choose enlightenment, from this Not Knowing.

"So," Junpo continued, "if you don't know who you are, then who are you?"

"I don't know," I repeated, deeply in shock but he shook his head.

"Slow this way, way down, baba. Who are you if you don't know who you are? You're not love, or awareness, or awakening, or emptiness, or the void, or God, or any of that fucking shit." He raised his eyebrows and his intensity went up a few degrees. It was uncomfortable.

I nodded.

"Who are you?" He almost growled the words at me.

I was barely able to stay inside of the intensity of the question. "I don't know."

"*You just fucking said that! GO DEEPER!*" He was speaking loudly, intensely, right into my face.

"I don't fucking know!" I shouted. Anger, my go-to emotion, was front and center in an instant. Junpo not only didn't flinch, he leaned in closer to me.

"Go *all the way* into it."

I shuddered. The tears came again, but this time I didn't bother to hide them. Suddenly I was the Not Knowing itself; I was the Great Mystery the mystics talk about, the Thing That Cannot Be Named. I was God outside of any human understanding of God; I was the ultimate subjectivity, a singular view out into the cosmos seeing itself. I was what existed before the Big Bang, and I was what will come after the Big Crunch. I was the Alpha and the Omega. I was everything because I was nothing. I didn't exist because I was everything, including this tiny little ego that had flashed into existence for a nanosecond, this little, tiny and utterly insignificant creature called *Keith* who, in a universe billions upon billions of years old, had been alive for a few decades.

It was hilarious, actually. A smile of wonderment crept onto my face and tears, now of joy, slid down my cheeks. "*Not Knowing,*" I breathed. "Not Knowing. *I am the Not Knowing!*"

"*You're* not *anything*," he corrected, his voice now gentle, but he looked deeply satisfied. "*Language is so important* here, baba, so important because it will matter in the next few hours and days as you integrate this. *You are not anything.*" He smiled. "Drop the 'I.' Who are you?"

"*Not Knowing.*" The words dropped between us like an anvil falling over—solid, certain, unmovable. I knew I had never uttered a single, truer thing in my entire life.

"Not knowing," he repeated, one of his wry little smiles coming to the corner of his mouth. He clapped a big hand onto my shoulder. "Good work."

I exhaled.

"Now," he said, picking up the mallet and ringing the bowl between us. "Shall we continue?"

The first step to choosing awakening is to get in touch with the Not Knowing at your core. By choosing to face this and experience this, you can take a big step toward a view beyond ego.

The question then arises: *Who chooses awakening?* And then, *Who awakens?* These are koans for you to answer with the depth of your insight, not with the breadth of your knowledge.

UNDERSTANDING THE CHOICE

The meditation practices later in this chapter may give you a taste of the nondual, or the experience of you and the thing you are viewing being not-two. Some might refer to this as unity consciousness, dhyana mind, rigpa, sahaj samadhi, or turiyatita. In a world that teaches us that we're here and the world is there, a nondual view shows us that no, there is only one view, and it is undivided, utterly. As an experience, this is profound. As an idea, it is fodder for debate among philosophers that would put most of us to sleep.

As a teacher of Zen, I've encountered more than one student who is stuck on this idea: There is a relative truth, which is to be shunned, and an absolute truth, which is the goal of one's spiritual practice. This very idea is, of course, dualistic. There is only one view and the illusion of a second, relative one. This doesn't mean the relative one isn't compelling or defensible or seemingly real, in the same way that optical illusions convince us that something we are seeing is real.

The idea of a relative and absolute view can become ideas not tethered to our experience, and therefore just another thing in the way of our genuine insight.

Right now, you can easily touch into a dualistic view. You're there, holding a book or reading on a screen or listening to this, which seems outside of you. It also seems obvious I wrote this at some point in your past, as an entirely separate human being. You are aware that you were born and you will die. *Etcetera.* If you just get a toe into a so-called absolute view, then it seems like the absolute is a different view than the one you have, and that you need to somehow set down your dualistic view and pick up an absolute one. This concept, of your existing dualistic view and of an absolute one where nothing is separated *as an experience of reality*, can get students very confused. It sets them on the path of seeking, of trying to uncover, discover, or somehow get to the absolute, *which is fully present right now inside of your seemingly dualistic view*. This becomes instantly obvious when your insight is deep enough and happens over a long enough period of time, but it is frustratingly impossible to see until you do. This is why this is an insight and not a piece of knowledge to be learned and studied and debated and analyzed. It is just so.

It is because of this confusion that for centuries Zen teachers have refused to give their students a map, instead forcing them to sit, sometimes in agony and confusion, to discover the territory for themselves. The trouble with giving students a map is it can be like watching a documentary on New York City. You can watch a dozen documentaries on New York but that's not the same as knowing the city intimately. Knowing the smells of the East Village in the summertime as you walk through Tompkins Square Park. Or the flush of air as you descend into the subway on a warm afternoon, expecting to find coolness underground but instead getting the hot breath of the New York City subway system. There's the ease of popping into an art gallery on the way to lunch, or catching a live jazz show when walking home from a friend's apartment on a Tuesday night.

Experiencing these things gives you a feel for the soul of a city that a documentary can never convey. The documentary can remind you of what you already know in your being, but we would not go to the person who watched the dozen documentaries on New York and ask them about their impressions of the city, for they have none of their own. The same could be said for someone who spent just a few hours in the city.

It is the same with nonduality. The potential problem with speaking about the nondual is most people have only heard about it or visited it very briefly, yet too often presume they are experts based on their very limited experience. This can create another idea that can only be overcome with a prolonged and deep exposure to awareness as awareness—not more books, or more talk, or more self-reflection. A nondual view isn't a philosophy, set of beliefs, organizing principle, or concept. It is born out of the direct perception of the world as it is, now. This view, from awareness as awareness, sees all good and evil, and very best and the very worst of humankind, as perfect manifestations of God, or spirit, or suchness, or emptiness, or fullness. There is no difference between the relative and the absolute, meaning that everything in every direction is equally spirit. There is no difference between heaven and earth, God and man, the ancestor realms and our realm, the ethereal and the material, elders and children, the rapist and the raped, the moral and the amoral, a clean environment or a dying one, or any other perceived duality.

This is why, in our practice, we allow what is—because what is, is spirit, God, enlightenment. The bad thoughts, the good thoughts, the saintly ideas, and the sinful lusting.

Suzuki Roshi said: "Nothing to see here, nothing to attain. Nothing except this moment, and all it contains." And by "all" he does, in fact, mean all—not most, not all except the parts we don't like, or all except for Hitler, sex trafficking, and systemic sexism, no—all.

You might on a warm and sunny summer afternoon be looking at something, say a creek, watching the bubbling water roll past you. Maybe your toes are dipped into the water, and you're a little sweaty from walking. Your shirt sticks to the small of your back, and you swat at some bugs flying around you. You're watching that water flow by, seeing the endless undulations of the current against the rocks formed millions of years ago, which are gradually being worn away on a scale so vast you are unable to imagine it.

And then, in a moment—you are the water, the rocks, the sun, and the sky, all. You're no longer looking at them—you are them. Everything is somehow the same, except there is no "I" any longer, there is no world "out there" being viewed by "you." And it is simply impossible to feel neurotic attachment to any of your thoughts or feelings, which may still come and go like the flies come and go and the water comes and goes, fine as they are because they're you-not-you. Things that once seemed life-and-death important suddenly just *are*. You might burst into laughter as you swat at yourself in the form of a fly. And if this perception lingers, if you get up and find your way back to your car that is you, and drive on a road that is you, and enter back into a stream of life that was once hilariously "yours" but now just is, you might find that some things require your heartfelt attention and other things do not. Yet your *attachment* to them, to being right, to being

CAN YOU CHOOSE ENLIGHTENMENT?

heard, to fixing the world, has vanished utterly, because from here there is no resisting that which you are. Resisting is just a game of the ego, the false but very entertaining dance of dualism. From this space, you see as clearly as the sun that warms your skin that the world no longer needs to be saved from itself because it is as it is and it can be no other way.

Maybe you know this place, and maybe you don't. It doesn't really matter except to say that once you experience it, there is no objection any longer to what is written here.

"But…" I often hear someone objecting, "does that mean I just sit back and watch the world burn with a stupid, smug, enlightened expression on my face?"

Notice the contraction away from what is into the egoic need to fix, change, alter, control, resist. Not in a "Oh, how stupid of you to ask," kind of way, but in a, "Notice the ego doing what it is meant to do," kind of way. The objection itself is rooted not here, now, but in a perceived future where, somehow, you won't be able to control your life any longer.

After a sustained enlightening, you may find that some things require your heartfelt attention, but that attention will be provided from a place of accepting the world as it is and working within what is without the need to resist it. Resistance, while great for bumper stickers and high school students looking to get a rise from their teachers, is not a sophisticated manner of fixing anything. Even if you go to war against the Nazis as a necessity to save the world from them, it can be from a place of acceptance and not resistance to what is.

Change can be very effective when you let go of the need to be a change *agent*, because it's *no longer about you* and what you want. When you see the world as it is you cannot help but weep at the suffering that is here.

As I've described, Junpo once was literally taken to his knees because he saw a tree that had been just cut down, saw it bleeding sap, bleeding out life force. He spoke about feeling anger at what was being done to the environment and dropping under the noise to the clarity underneath. He cared about the state of the world and the sentient beings within it, and then he used his meditation practice to experience the truth of his not being separate from those things being hurt or from those doing the hurting. Reality, undivided, allowed him to experience the world as both the perpetrated and the perpetrator, both, and from a place of compassion, he stepped forward as an environmentalist. He spent his life using humor and playfulness to show others the importance of environmental stewardship without making some people bad and other people good. Zen, you may recall, is beyond good and evil, beyond right and wrong.

You have a choice to make.

Do you choose to allow the truth of the not knowing at the core of your being to be experienced?

Are you willing to live a minute, an hour, a day, or a lifetime as not knowing itself?

If so, you may experience the nature of the nondual, which can be very challenging for an ego to fully allow. Opinion and awakening are mutually exclusive states. Ask yourself: Would the world be a more peaceful place if more people were no longer attached to their opinions? Would you be a more peaceful person if you were no longer so attached to your opinions?

REMINDERS ABOUT CHOOSING

It should be getting clearer that the nature of choosing enlightenment isn't as simple as choosing lunch. I would like to add in four more reminders about the nature of an awakened mind, which we've already covered in this book, but that are important to repeat.

There's Nothing to Get

It's extraordinarily challenging to simply allow what is here to arise. As said repeatedly throughout this book, it seems like enlightenment is something that we *get* and so it makes sense that we approach a spiritual practice like we approach any other kind of practice, where some version of *energy + time invested = results*. The problem is it doesn't work this way in the spiritual game. Practice alone won't awaken you. Most of the teachers who advocate for "just waking up" are speaking from their direct experience. They see, after their own breakthroughs, that their practice seemed to not be doing anything. There was no practice that "caused" their awareness to appear, nothing they *did* that actually created a transition to "awake." The lack of emphasis on practice is, therefore, understandable. Remember that in Zen we call awakening the gateless gate, because once through it you see there was never any gate there to begin with. And yet practice, for almost everyone, seems necessary to prepare us for the obliterating insights that come from an awakened view.

Liberation Is through Life, Not from It

Being with *what is* also means being with your full humanness. There's no getting away from your childhood conditioning (although it can be understood and transformed with time), your cultural conditioning, your biological conditioning, your unseen shadows, or the many other ways you're not really running the ship of you.

Coming fully into *the now* can sometimes mean coming fully into a feeling of terror or fear, or a deep depression, or the searing grief of loss. Being with what is means being *fully* with our human emotions as they arise, something that is very hard for most of us to do. Most spiritual people believe that enlightenment takes you off the wheel of suffering, which it most certainly does not. You are no longer bound to the wheel or bound to the suffering and, therefore, you no longer resist it—but you're not free of it, either. You're free of your attachment to things being other than what they are. This is a different kind of freedom than most imagine spiritual masters to have. This is what you're choosing, not to go to go some faraway place where you're off the wheel of your humanity. That place simply does not exist, and the idea of such a place is the prison in which most practitioners bind themselves.

Integrating Spiritual Insight Takes Time

Spiritual experiences or transformations, no matter how sudden and profound, still need to be understood, interpreted, integrated, and verbalized through existing ego structures, and those structures are fully human and fully fallible, all the way up (to your highest self) and all the way down (to your most base trauma). The sudden realization that you are what you seek is different from the stable and permanent integration of that truth. No matter how strong or instant a realization, it will still need to be integrated into your life, your ego view, and your day-to-day existence.

Awakening doesn't automatically transform the conditioning of your ego. Even if it was possible, spiritual insights would still need to be understood through an ego. If your conditioned mind, your everyday mind, which has a lot of trauma and neurosis inside of it (and most of ours do), you may very well find a deep and genuine spiritual insight gets corrupted if you presume that spiritual insight can root out your psychological shadow (more on this in the Postscript on sexual and other kinds of abuse by teachers). This can be especially true around things where shadow tends to linger, like sex, power, intimate relationships, and money—all things better explored with your therapist than a meditation master.

Enlightenment Is Disruptive

No one really knows why some people awaken and others don't. Someone once said, "Enlightenment is an accident. And meditation makes you accident-prone."[30] It seems like the majority of meditation practices don't lead their practitioners to a stable and permanent realization, and yet those who have had a practice, and end up seeing the world as awakening itself, seem to be able to allow the realization to take hold more deeply and more quickly than those who don't have a practice. Speaking from experience, the process of awakening can be highly disruptive. If you have been training your mind under a meditation master who understands what this process can be like, day in and day out, it's seems to be easier when the insights come, because those insights will shatter your ideas of the world and yourself.

---

[30] This quote has been attributed to many different teachers, but its truthfulness has been cited by many, from Ken Wilber to Baker Roshi.

CHOOSING ENLIGHTENMENT

We've come to it at last. How to choose enlightenment. There are only four simple steps here, which I suggest you first bring fully and completely into a meditation practice. When you find you can do these four practices on your cushion with relative ease, you can begin to practice them off of your cushion and in the world at-large. Junpo used to love to say that meditation never ends.

The First Step: Allow Everything

Often in a meditation practice we try to be what we imagine is a "good meditator." Just like how I started out this book, with spiritual people preferring one half of the world and hating the other half, we too are the same way in our practice. We think that our meditation practice should be still, and profound, illuminated, and effortless. And in believing these things we push away or resist those parts of ourselves that don't fit into that nice conception of what meditation should be.

The first step, therefore, in sitting down in your practice is a simple phrase: *Allow everything, resist nothing.*

This phrase, when you really act on it, can free the part of your mind that is trying to do things right, and that defines its existence by trying to fix anything (or anyone) that isn't right. If you accept everything and resist nothing, certain kinds of thoughts will not bother you, such as the self-bullying notions ("You can't shut up for five seconds!"), parental admonitions ("You really should find a teacher. You can't do this on your own!"), or hopeless criticism ("You've literally wasted the last twenty minutes thinking about lunch!"). If you allow everything and resist nothing, then two things can happen. At first, you will allow these self-critical thoughts to arise without any resistance. And then, after a few weeks or months, those thoughts may simply cease to arise at all.

Remember that when the ego tries to overpower the ego, all you get is war. This is why you must allow *everything* inside of your practice. You allow, because the grand, ultimate truth of the universe must, by definition, include your discursive and disruptive thoughts, those where you're not spiritually mature enough, your self-doubt, your raging emotions, and your lack of discipline. You allow *what already is* to simply be, radically. Even slipping out of the practice is still part of the practice itself. You are awake and liberated no matter if you know it or not, so all of your struggles and all of your resistance to that reality is awake and liberated, too. It's a paradox that takes a leap of faith to realize, great doubt to stabilize, and great perseverance to integrate.

Allow everything, resist nothing.

You are, by definition, aware of anything that you can witness arising inside of your awareness. For instance, you can see and recognize your hand on your body; therefore, you're more than just your hand. In this manner, you start by noticing your physical, gross body, especially the chest and belly. What's happening there, what might they say if they could talk? What sensations are arising, what pleasure or pains? You are more than just your body that you're watching arise, breath to breath.

You then move to your emotions. What does it feel like today, in this moment, being you? Is there heartbreak, or irritation, or happiness, or anger? Perhaps boredom? Tiredness? Weariness? Anxiety or depression, longing, or exhaustion? What is the emotional landscape of you as you begin your practice? We are more than just our feelings.

Then to your thoughts. What is your mind like today, in this moment? Critical? Fast or slow? Sluggish? Sharp, or maybe open and relaxed? Yet here you are, more than just your thoughts that you are watching arise.

Not just thoughts, not just feelings, not just a body.

Then to your "big thoughts" or "complicated thoughts." These might include the historical idea of "you"—your hard-earned identity, your firmly-held opinions, your sense of where you're so right about things, the deeply carved neuronal grooves that define how you organize the endless data and sensations that we call reality. You're more than your identity, your beliefs, your opinions, your valuations, your fears, and your stories about the world, even if you're convinced those stories are "right."

Just for the practice, notice that your true identity lies beyond these constructs. You are the *not knowing* underneath all of that, the Great Mystery itself. You were never born and you will never die, because you're not of this place and yet you are every single part of this place. Since you don't know who you are, don't worry about what your identity might be; for now, just rest in all the things you know *you are not*, which is anything you can see, name, or recognize.

Allow everything, resist nothing.

The Second Step: There's Nothing Wrong Here

The spiritual teacher Reggie Ray tells a story of working with his teacher, Chögyam Trungpa Rinpoche. The two of them were in a room together when an attendant appeared to tell Reggie some terrible news: His father had suddenly died. In deep shock (his father had been healthy), Reggie turned to his teacher, who simply said, "There's no problem here." It stopped Reggie's racing mind and his sense of shock, because the shock was centered around that very idea that something was *very* wrong. Trungpa's words stuck with him with the force of a fist and ended up transforming how Reggie experienced that pivotal death. He went from being in resistance to what was to embracing it with the totality of his being. Grief came faster, harder, and was processed through, not around.

There's no problem here.

Only a madman or a spiritual master would dare say that to someone who had just lost a parent. And of course, Trungpa was a bit of both.

Nothing is wrong here. This is a second, powerful thing you can remind yourself as you sit down to meditate:

- Allow everything, resist nothing.
- There's nothing wrong here.

This second phrase helps to counteract a strong bias of the human animal. The human brain is wired to notice what's wrong around us, from our own thoughts, to our home, to our partner, to our world. This "negativity bias" has been well documented in psychology, and it's very likely one of the reasons we've been a successful species, so far.[31] This can make meditation an

---

31 https://www.ncbi.nlm.nih.gov/pmc/articles/PMC3652533

interesting experience, because one of the main things we evolved to do is scan for what's wrong so we can fix it.

In your meditation, you might suddenly notice that the wall needs paint, that you haven't finished your taxes, or that you're not sure your partner really meant it fully when she said *I love you* that morning. As your mind begins to quiet down, the first thing you may experience is all the things that aren't right in the world, with you, with your practice, with your dog, with your cat, with your parents, with your country, with your environment, with your culture, with your car, with your friendships, with your creative self-expression…it can be quite a list.

Sometimes you'll get up and go fix what you think needs fixing—send that text or order that thing online. Or sometimes, you'll stop one kind of meditation practice and find another kind of meditation that can fix what's "wrong" with the practice. The teacher Adyashanti likes to say that 95 percent of the people who come to him have, at heart, the same question: How do I get away from this moment?

In truth, we all know how to get out of and away from this moment, because that's mostly what our lives are. What if it could be another way for you? What if you could be with life, as it is, as if there *was nothing wrong here*?

Simply come back to the practice, come back to a simple concentration, and allow even the thought that you're not doing it right to come, and to go, perfect as-is.

There's nothing wrong here.

Tell yourself this simple phrase when you feel especially fed up with yourself. Then act as if that *might be* true and see what that makes possible.

The Third Step: There's Nothing Right Here

This is a very hard concept for some. Most understand the power *of there's nothing wrong here* because it gives your ego permission to relax the self-critical parts that it tends to throw at itself and at the world at large. It helps your ego to relax more into what is. Yet *this* one can be very hard for an ego to say and believe. Again, if that's the case with you, just try it on *inside of your practice.* See if it can open doors of perception that once were firmly barred to you.

We live in a curious time when so many of us are being asked to *assert our knowing* into the world, from our friends to social media to our children. Asserting our knowing can be a very good thing, of course, because it helps to ensure that buildings don't fall down and bridges don't collapse, that we can find a competent surgeon or plumber (or be one), and can assure our children that the sun, not the earth, is the center of our solar system.

We get into more trouble, however, when we get firmly *attached* to our knowing. Western medicine, for instance, can have real trouble with its close-minded attachment to being the best and only "real" form of treatment. Pundits make their living off their attachment to their view against the "other" side. Social media is almost nothing but attachment to asserting one's knowing. Conspiracies of all kinds of silly things exist, from flat earth to QAnon, where people are asserting their knowing in a very close-minded and absolutistic kind of way. *We all do it,* to be clear (not just "them"), but we can begin to let go of this process inside of our meditation practice.

The idea here is a simple one: You can't do your practice wrong, but you can't do it right, either. In other words, in your meditation you let go of the deep human need to *valuate* everything, and instead just let your practice be your practice, without getting attached to the idea that you might be doing it right or wrong. Another powerful saying of Junpo's was, "God does not share your valuations." (That's a koan, by the way.)

If you stop valuating, which means if you give up the idea that you can do your practice right, then in the space this lack of valuation may begin to give you a glimpse of what's here, now: a deep and ever-present awareness, looking out from the Great Mystery of your eyes and as your eyes, to the world and as the world, seeing all and valuating nothing. If that's true, how could anything be wrong here? Or right? They are two sides of a single valuation.

There's nothing right here.

This phrase can be helpful when you've had an especially rich and profound and still meditation, the kind your ego will be tempted to categorize as *good*, to valuate as the kind of meditation that is desirable, sought after, and nourishing. That would put you back into a world where you desire and value part of what's arising, and resist the things arising that you don't like. A so-called bad meditation can be as rich and powerful as a so-called good meditation, if you hold that *there's nothing right here*.

To break the spell of our valuating mind, we must be willing to let go of both sides of our attachment: the clearly hard and difficult meditations where it seems like nothing is right, and the mystical and transcendent meditations where is seems like everything is right. They are merely two sides of one coin, and you're invited to set the coin down altogether.

The Fourth Step: Pure Listening

You've taken your seat. You've sat down on a cushion or in a chair. You've:

- Agreed that you have and are that which you seek.
- Chosen to allow everything and resist nothing.
- Allowed that there's nothing wrong here.
- Allowed that there's nothing right here.

Now pay attention to your ears. Some sound is arising right now. Maybe you're in a café and you hear the murmurs of the people around you, or the drone of a jet engine as you sit on a plane, or the sound of a bird chirping or a creek running past. A TV in another room, cars outside, a noisy neighbor, a lawn mower, traffic. If you notice, sound comes into your ears without you *doing* anything. It just arises, and it arises in your mind, at least at first, without any thoughts, feelings, or valuations of any kind.

You might ask: *Who is listening?*

Listening happens before thought and feeling, as we've observed. Listening as pure awareness can be the locus of your practice if you allow sound to arise, and observe as it does. Listen and notice with all your being. You can't stop the sound through an act of will, but you can witness the sound, and so you're more than just the sound. If you listen with all your being, you'll hear the sound in the deepest part of yourself, in the part that is beyond and below thought, feeling, identity, belief, or valuation. There is pure listening inside of pure awareness, and you can experience it in this very moment for yourself.

You listen from your Not Knowing, and from the Great Mystery. You *valuate* that listening from your ego, from your consciousness, but you listen from Not Knowing. And so, right now, you can touch into the Not Knowing by choosing to listen with the totality of your being, while asking yourself this simple question: *Who listens?*

Listening is the foundation of my practice. Just listening. Online meditation apps often have random bells you can set up to listen to as they arise and fall away. They might shock you into noticing you've been caught up in thinking, and the sound of the bell will bring you back into a gentle listening and being with what is. There is, at the core of your being, something that is capable of just purely listening. This is awareness itself, so simple, and so obvious and close at hand that it's very easy to miss. What is arising for you now, in this very moment, and who is listening to it?

When this becomes easier, you can do the same practice, but this time act as if you're listening with your heart, not with your ears. It's as if you had a big ear sticking out of your chest, and sounds go into there instead of into your ears on your head. I don't want to talk too much about this practice because I want it to surprise you. Try the listening exercise but with an intention to listen with your heart and see what that may cause to come alive.

ARE YOU ENLIGHTENED?

You will know awareness is looking out at the world as awareness because it will be obvious. Pure awareness is so fundamentally different from our most expanded or spiritual-feeling *states of consciousness* that there is no mistaking it any more than you might accidentally miss falling in love with someone. It is quite literally that obvious and that impactful. It's quite impossible to miss and quite challenging to describe.

Many years back, as Junpo and I were writing *The Heart of Zen*, we sat down with a video camera. He agreed to let me ask him anything I wanted, without him knowing first what the questions might be. One of my questions to him was, "How does someone know if they're enlightened?"

"Because you'll break out laughing!" he said, laughing himself. "And you'll get the joke—you'll know you're awake because nothing—nothing—

can disturb your *wah* [essence]. Because you're fundamentally *awake*—and awake comes back to Buddhism 101: Bud equals awake. It means you see through the myth of your evaluating mind. It means you see through your ego. You recognize that before Christ, before Gautama Buddha, before Abraham, you are." He paused again, his eyes turning inward for a moment.

"And that's a humbling place. It's not some narcissistic 'I'm awake' place. It's like, 'Oh my God, *this is who I am!*' And then what? Do you surrender and serve and alleviate suffering, or do you walk above it all? Interesting dilemma, when you finally become awake."

If you're thinking he was implying it is *better* to serve and surrender to alleviate suffering rather than *walking above it all*, your insight is not deep enough. God does not share your valuations.

Once you experience the nondual for yourself and as yourself, when you see it with your own eyes and feel it inside of your own heart, it is obvious that we don't wake up. We don't become enlightened. We simply realize that part of us is already awake, that God is closer to us than we are to ourselves. And so there's nothing special to claim, no need to take up the mantel of a spiritual teacher, no need to put on a roshi's robes and shave one's head, and certainly no need to begin to sell water down by the river.

This truth changes completely how we practice because we no longer try and quiet the mind—we allow the quietness that's already here. We don't try and awaken the mind—we simply allow the awakening that is already here. And we certainly don't try and be spiritual people—we simply allow the love and compassion that are arising out of our being in this moment to be fully liberated from any sense of morality or ethics whatsoever.

PUTTING IT ALL TOGETHER TO LET IT ALL GO

There is no practice that can liberate you—no secret, ancient practice of the Tibetans, nor some long-hidden practice of the Hindus. There are no profound practices saved for only the best students that will lead to awakening as soon as one practices them. This is all more ego, more grasping, more valuating, more trying to find something that you already have.

CAN YOU CHOOSE ENLIGHTENMENT?

Every time you get triggered you have a chance to notice for yourself that your angst is your liberation. Before thinking, before reacting, before sensation, there is awareness. You're not aware, you're conscious, but under your consciousness is awareness, perfectly aware. Can you feel into it now, in this moment? If not, when's the next time you'll get triggered by something? Remind yourself so that when it happens, you can see awareness is here, first, before you react.

Awakening doesn't and can't awaken your shadows, your traumas, your attachment disorders, your childhood conditioning, your ego, or your cultural conditioning. These things stay, and the awareness that is aware gets expressed through the warped lens of the impermanent self. That lens is always warped because it is a human one. Beware of this in your own practice and beware of any teacher who claims to be fully awakened and fully beyond their own shadows. None are, and the ones who think they are can be doing great harm to their students.

Choose to slow down.

Choose to listen to your mind and your body, and to the world that seems to be outside of yourself.

Choose to let your attention be with all that's arising inside of you and around you. And maybe, just maybe, as you make that choice the veil will slip away and you'll find yourself without a self at all, liberated and free and simply awake and aware, instead of opinionated and asleep.

Choose to not do anything at all except watch the glorious unfolding of what is.

Choose to experience the truth that you don't need to be free of the wheel of life and death because there is nothing to be freed from. The wheel of life and death arises and falls away inside of this very mind, this very moment. Life isn't beautiful or terrible. It just is.

Choose to sit with these koans: What is this my life really about? What is the meaning of life and karma and birth and death?

The oak tree stump, bleeding in the courtyard. Nothing more, and nothing less.

CHAPTER 8

Enlightening

Junpo used to say that if you can't put an experience into words, then it never really happened for you. That is why he was so careful with language when he and I worked together, to make sure that I was imprinting things accurately into my memory. I'd like us to do the same here, and to summarize what we've considered in this book since it's full of some esoteric and complicated topics that may be hard to recall.

The promise of this book was to free yourself from yourself, so that you can, paradoxically, be fully human. We covered rich territory, including why your identity, so necessary to live and survive in the world, is actually merely a construct, a process, and not something that can deliver on what it seems to most want—namely, happiness and fulfillment.

Yet your identity, and the ego, are also not the enemy, something to be defeated and overcome in your earnest striving inside of a spiritual practice. This too is a false start and a dead end.

When we look at the self, we can see that it is entirely a construct. Our ideas of "I" have changed radically over the course of our lives, so that who we were at eight years old is vastly different from who we are at fifty. Most people never understand that who they think they are is merely their biological, psychological, and cultural conditioning. They live under an illusion of freedom, of a separate and whole person they think is solid and concrete. With this false idea of a solid and concrete self, they constantly carve reality, the endlessly infinite and infinitely creative stream of evolution, into packets they can understand, dominate, and seem to control with their opinions, rejecting the parts of reality they don't like and embracing the parts they do.

I say *they*, but the truth is we all do this in some ways. As a result, most of us are completely out of touch with the world as it is. Instead, we see our projections, opinions, valuations, stories, and reactions as "objective" reality and conflate one with the other. We love one half of the world and hate the other half, and we believe, somewhat hilariously, that we are the ultimate arbiter of what is right and what is wrong. *Climate change is bad! Abortion is terrible! War is horrible! Cultural appropriation is an abomination! The patriarchy needs to be crushed! Making us wear masks is fascist!* You believe yourself and justify your self-righteousness and resentment by resisting the parts of the world that don't conform to what you think is right.

And the whole time reality goes on, being real, and giving precisely zero fucks about your opinion of it. This is how the illusion of the self creates suffering within you and outside of you, as you rail and rage against what is. War is the result of a divided mind, either war against the self or war against others perceived to be enemies of what you think is real. And yet reality is undivided, whole, complete unto itself. It was here before you came into existence in your body-mind, and it will be here when you leave your body-mind. And yet, somehow, you think you know better than reality, know better than what is.

As stated many times in this book, this insight, this truth, isn't an excuse to fold your arms across your chest and watch the world burn, but it is a way to orient to how you engage in the change that might be needed—by accepting what is, first, and then working to create change, second.

The cause of your suffering is directly correlated to your lack of ability to discern your opinion and valuation from the reality in which you are utterly and completely immersed. You start to release this grip on the world by first admitting you're mostly conditioned. This can allow a crack in your awareness to see how you constrain and distort reality to your will, and this can allow you to see the places where you may be deeply and neurotically conditioned by your parents, your culture, and even by your body (cortisol and adrenaline, or an overactive amygdala).

As humans we can never be free of our conditioning, but we can get a sense of just how deeply it runs and, in so doing, begin to lessen its grip on our sense of self. That sense of self, you'll recall, is best thought of as a process and not a self.

A process is always in process, never stable, never static, highly mutable, changeable, malleable, prone to being influenced, often wrong, and always partial. You are a process and not a self and holding yourself as such can help you dislodge some of your stubborn attachment to being right all the time, which you most assuredly are not.

REAL VERSUS TRUE

Put simply, things can be very real that are not true. For instance, I can think the earth is flat. That is real to me, but it's obviously not true. In my own life story, I often found things to be psychologically real, like the impacts my childhood had on my ability to be in relationship. It seemed and was very real that my childhood experiences caused me to behave in all kinds of problematic ways throughout much of my life. And yet, as I've turned more deeply into myself in the ways outlined at the end of this book, I've come to discover a deeper truth: There are no external tormentors in my life. There is nothing outside of me that causes me to react in a way that makes it seem like the external trigger is making me do anything. I can no longer blame my mother, my educators, my culture, my upbringing, or anything else. The only place to look is within. Only I ever choose to react, and so only I am responsible for how I feel, how I act, and how I am in the world. That truth blows apart the realness of my childhood story and leaves me as the sole arbiter of my own life. There is no one with power over me but me, no matter what is happening in the external world.

The great Hindu sage Ramana Maharshi said that which is not present in deep, dreamless sleep is not real. In other words, the only thing present in deep, dreamless sleep is awareness itself, undifferentiated, unmoving, timeless, deathless, fearless, and eternal. Therefore the only thing real, the only thing true, is awareness itself *as itself*. This awareness sees and *is* the world as it arises in all its wholeness, including war, rape, environmental ruin, love, saints, puppies, spring days, a newborn infant cradled in his mother's arms, and child sex trafficking.

The world is as it is and it can be no other way. This can only be understood in the depths of your own practice and realization, for these are just words, just stupid concepts otherwise, ideas floating across the page that may or may not have any validity for you, no more or less real than Christ is the Lord or only Islam is the true way.

Only you can test what I claim here, for yourself, and discover what's real and what's true to you. The Buddha said to not believe teachers and to not believe teachings and, I'd follow, to not even believe that. Try on these practices for yourself, and see what gets illuminated in the part of you that is deeper than your ego, older than your personas, vaster than the sky itself, and more ancient than the most ancient stars shining above.

YOUR SPIRITUAL SELF

A spiritual self is an especially tricky identity. On the one hand, it can help you to get onto a spiritual path. Yet if that path isn't designed to show that the very identity itself isn't real, you'll quickly stall out and fire opinions out and into the world about what a spiritual person should be, how a spiritual person should act, and what a spiritual person should be experiencing. A spiritual identity only works when it is used as a way to free you from it, so that when you are resting in an enlightening view of the world and yourself, there is no spiritual self at all. You see, you experience, there is no self at all, *just a process*.

Having an identity of *spiritual* is just something else that needs to be set down on the path, which is part of why the one Chan master said, "*If you meet the Buddha on the path, kill him.*" Does this mean to actually kill your spiritual teacher? Of course not. But it does mean that your ideas of Buddhahood, your ideas of spirituality, need to be killed before you can become the Buddha you already are. Like so much in this book, this truth rests inside of a paradox that can only be resolved inside the depths of your own experience and being, just like you can only resolve the paradox of the Big Bang inside of your own insight, insight of the creative force that is arising within you, even now.

In places like Boulder, people get so attached to being spiritual they can't have insights deep enough to undermine that very identity. And so they get stuck, looking at the infinite arising of reality through the lens and the constraints of a "spiritual person," missing much of what is actually happening in the world and inside of themselves.

> *Who is hearing?*
> *Your physical being doesn't hear,*
> *nor does the Void.*
> *Then what does?*
> *Strive to find out!*
> *Put aside your rational intellect,*
> *give up all techniques,*
> *just get rid of the notion of self.*
> —Zen Master Bassui

SUCCESS OR FAILURE ON THE SPIRITUAL PATH

If you think you're playing a good spiritual game and are a good spiritual person, you are not. If your goal is to awaken fully from suffering, you must make a hard choice: You cannot be special and know the deepest truth of the universe. Those two things are mutually exclusive. If you can abandon your need to be special, you can know the deepest truth of existence by being that truth. But it will obliterate all you think you know and it might make the distinction between success and failure on the spiritual path something that is deeply, deeply amusing to you, since such distinctions cannot exist from the deepest part of your knowing. One of Junpo's favorite quips when working with people and helping them first get a glimpse of the undivided truth of existence was, "Ah, now we're getting nowhere!"

FUNDAMENTAL GOODNESS

When you meet some of the great, awakened teachers for yourself, you may be unsure what to make of them. These people are alive with life, full of strong views on the world, and often bursting with an irrational sense of goodness at this whole enterprise of existence. When you rest in an enlightened view, you don't look out at the world with a neutral and dispassionate stare, slobbering on a non-existence face. There is no external morality in the deepest parts of your knowing, but there is an internal goodness that is obvious, joyous, and unmistakable.

There is a reason I laughed with all of the major insights I had, and a reason I still do. Sitting in the truth is joyous. Junpo used to say that the first thing he experienced coming out of awareness was compassion. He couldn't explain it, but in his words if we are awakened, it is impossible to act selfishly. Not as a moral edict, but as an obvious, lived truth of our being. Because the fundamental nature of the universe is, somehow, goodness. Once again, this isn't a belief or an edict, and you should never take my word for it but instead see if it's true in the deepest part of your own being. After all, all I'm doing is selling water by the river. Go down and sample the river for yourself!

When we allow awareness, there is, as part of its construct, a fundamental goodness that opens the heart and lifts the spirit. I don't know why this is the case, but I do know it is so. For while awakening can and will obliterate your sense of self, it will also open you to a joy and a lightness, and a sense of the fundamental goodness of all that is, without exception. This is why you can then be with all that is, including the seemingly bad things in the world. You come to see all of manifest existence (and I do mean *all*) as children of the universe, dancing in perfection, moving from nothing and back into nothing but leaving something beautiful as they move, as evolution evolves, as the universe wakes to itself, as these thinking monkeys differentiate from all around them only to integrate back into *the all*. The world is out of your control. You are out of your control. Don't you get that? How much more evidence will you need until you can admit this truth and be surrendered to Great Mystery *as* the Great Mystery?

The only sensible path is to surrender to *what is* rather than fight it. Or you can keep doing what you've always done, which is to uselessly, passionately, and hilariously rail against reality, throwing yourself again and again against the door trying to break it down, to bend it to your will, not knowing that when you finally break through you'll simply find yourself on the other side.

It's your choice to make. It has always been your choice to make, and it always will be. It's not mine, or your teacher's, or your karma's. It's yours, and it can be no other way. When you realize this, you laugh and come to understand that you can act on this world with this fundamental goodness as your driver, and you can do so without being attached to your actions aimed at saving the world from itself. The world always remains out of your control, but you can be free within it, if you so choose.

POSTSCRIPT

My Dark Night of the Self

This book is about being with what is, in all dimensions of our being. From this view, there is information in our feelings that can allow us to understand our conditioning on a much deeper level. We can begin, although never finish, the process of waking up from our conditioned selves. To put it more simply: Awakening includes the whole of you (and me, and the world). That must include all of your traumas, repressions, attachment disorders, personality quirks, neurotic tendencies, self-destructive habits, selfish proclivities, and every other single thing you don't like or can't see about yourself. Enlightenment, according to the great Zen master Dogen, is intimacy with all things. And that must include all of us, "warts and all," as my grandmother used to say.

As this book unfolded, a string of remarkable events took place—events that challenged my own ability to be radically with *what is*. There was the pandemic, of course. And Trump and the nearly insanely heated American politics of his era. There was George Floyd and the increasing rancor over a racial reckoning in the United States. The most intimate relationship of my life up to that point came crashing to an end in a way that was deeply shocking to me. Junpo, my beloved teacher, died after a years-long decline. My parents moved out of the house in which I was born, and it was sold to a new family. And my own trauma, from childhood and adolescence, erupted into my life in ways impossible to ignore—wrecking my sleep, disrupting my ability to work, encouraging me to find solace at the bottom of a wine bottle, and eventually leading me into the depth of controversial ketamine-assisted psychotherapy.

During this past year, being with *what is* was the last thing I wanted to do. Still, after years of relative peace in the emotional realm, a very strange incident caused me to realize that my inner work was far from complete. As the pandemic began in March of 2020, I was in the third year of a loving and committed partnership, one in which I had, for the first time in my life, learned to fully embrace, holding none of myself back. My lifelong habit of allowing my avoidant attachment to rule had been successfully metabolized. I would have followed my then-partner to the ends of the earth, and I loved her in a reckless way that I had never allowed before.

Since the details are less relevant than their impact, and since this is my story and not hers, I'll simply say that I found that she was out of integrity regarding a shared and important agreement in our partnership, a lapse of integrity I discovered. Finding this out was like an atom bomb going off in my heart. We had an intense conversation about it. I was totally dissociated from what I was really feeling, and badly so. I was really talking more at her, not to her, and at some point she asked me a simple question: *"Is this giving you what you need?"*

I allowed the question inside of me and watched as it showed me the very clear answer. "No," I admitted to myself as much to her.

"What do you need, then?" she asked, lovingly.

And in a second, I burst into uncontrollable tears, mumbling to myself things I'd picked up from my childhood. *I'll give you something to cry about! Knock it off!* Some part of me was desperate to stop the crying. *Stop it! Stop it! Stop it!* And my right hand, seemingly possessed, rose up and struck me across my own cheek, repeatedly and savagely. I was unable to stop it, and these two selves, the one crying and the one trying to stop the crying, fought for some kind of control as the witnessing part of myself watched. It was by far the most terrifying thing I've ever experienced because for a stretch of

MY DARK NIGHT OF THE SELF

time, I was completely out of control. She came to me and gently put her hand on my knee. "Please stop," I heard, as if from another room. Eventually I did. The next day I woke up and was unsure why my jaw was bruised and my mouth ragged. It was only when she asked me, later in the day, about the previous night that I realized I had repressed it completely, and the whole of the memory came crashing back into view along with horror at both the repression and the act of self-violence.

In the days and weeks that followed, I had no way to understand what happened to me, or even how to understand it. That attack on myself was very obviously pointing to deeper shadows and highlighting ways that I've always had proclivities toward self-destructive behavior, including self-hatred and self-abuse. Some part of me seemed to hate some other part of me, at a minimum, but who all these parts were, when they were formed, and *what they needed* were all mysteries. It didn't help that the pandemic crashed down on us, increasing the pressure. A few months later, my relationship with my partner ended suddenly and shockingly (to me) and predictably (to her). Yet it was without rancor, blame, or finger-pointing.

That was when I turned into what was here.

The way out is through, and going back through my childhood trauma was not an easy path. I spent many nights nearly sleepless, was prone to constant anxiety, and had more than one powerful panic attack. I was able to see how my partner had presented me with an impossible situation: She had hurt me and betrayed my trust, and then that very same day she had been able to open me up to the great sadness and vulnerability at that betrayal—emotions that wanted to stay hidden under a layer of anger and self-righteousness and lifelong conditioning because I didn't, of course, trust her. And for some protective, young part of myself, having the vulnerability exposed, to the very person who caused it, was simply intolerable. That "protector" did what he thought was the best thing to do, namely beat the vulnerable part back inside where, paradoxically, he could protect it. This is the kind of strange inner landscape you can discover if your childhood is veined with trauma, and you choose to climb all the way back into it. There be monsters there.

As the dark summer and fall of 2020 wore on, my mind was practiced enough, and my insight deep enough, that I was able to stay connected to the undivided reality, to source, even in the midst of these great moments of pain, but there were days when my sense of self was itself seen through as a construct. When I saw through all of the selves that made up "Keith," and when I saw that they were all constructed but none of them were really true, a feeling of deep terror arose, for there was no self to organize reality or to hold the trauma that was coming through "me." For a time, there was no self to do the work of integrating the selves, just a viewless view and a steady stream of trauma selves and unfiltered emotion, all bursting through the surface of my being. It was by far the hardest and most challenging thing I've ever experienced.

Yet another paradox, though: My day-to-day life was much the same as always. I worked, and wrote, and interacted with friends and family. Only an inner circle knew the reality of what I was facing, and the darkness and terror that would sometimes arise in overpowering ways. Through ketamine therapy, the help of two gifted therapists, the support of my men's group, and the love of two special humans to whom I grew very close, the shadows gradually came to light. I had to practice what I was preaching in this book, which meant turning into all of this, fully. Allowing all of this, fully. Experiencing everything and avoiding nothing. Turning into panic, fully. Sitting on my meditation cushion when I was indescribably exhausted and afraid, but choosing to sit there and face what was, as fully as I was able. More fear, more contraction, less sleep, for months and months, until slowly a deeper understanding began to emerge, a deeper integration, a deeper capacity to see what was real, and what was *true*. (The two are not the same thing, at all. A five-year-old might believe that the moon follows her as she walks—that is real to her, but it is not, in fact, true.)

Due to my childhood circumstances, I had learned to hide my vulnerability beginning at a young age. Tears and "weakness" were dangerous and never welcome, and for most of my adult life I unconsciously hid my vulnerability under a persona of detached aloofness—the Zen priest, the martial arts master, the motorcyclist. My relationship with my then-partner had successfully shattered my aloofness in our love for each other, and she had skillfully pressed me to go deeper when I was talking *at* her that night and not *to* her.

Complex, yes. But in my experience, no more complex than any one of us. In the years since, I've learned much about the inner workings of my personas and how they operate inside of me, seeing where they create realities that are not, in fact, true. I've slowly, haltingly, and carefully peeled back the layers of my selves to see what's really here, and to be fully with what I find.

Being with what is has meant uncovering those voices inside of me, frozen in time and in my psyche, stagnant and generating all kinds of shadow behaviors from me over the years.

As I've continued my practices of just sitting, I've also continued the practice of getting to know these old selves—talking to them, listening to them, valuing them, and inviting them into the larger container of this self of me that itself is just a construct, a temporary way of organizing the wonder of existence that continuously and spontaneously unfolds from moment to moment. My Keith-ness, after all, is no truer than my personas forged in childhood. He is just a temporary construct of self that came into existence and will, one day, go out of existence.

There is no awakening from the wheel of life. You can only awaken *on* the wheel of life, when you can see that the freedom is in being with *what is*, including the mess and the mire as much as the beautiful and the transcendent. Freedom is intimacy with all things, especially those monsters inside who, when you look long enough, turn out to be children, hiding with their hands over their vulnerable and beautiful and curious faces. Behind them, you find your own true face before you were born. The limitless and endlessly creative Great Mystery that you are not, and yet is all that you are.

Acknowledgments

Writing a book is never a project done by oneself. I am indebted to many. First and foremost to my teacher, Junpo Roshi who, despite his recent death, continues to teach me in a myriad of ways. Robb Smith of Integral Life was infinitely patient as I struggled with a title that we both liked, and I'm deeply grateful for his trust in me and in this book. Suz Byers and Mark Michael Lewis offered invaluable feedback on early drafts of the manuscript. My men's group—Casey, William, Joel, Huy, Marco, Bryce, and Robert—helped me through some of my darkest days after the death of Junpo and the end of a long-term relationship. Suz Byers and Kat Sullivan provided emotional, practical, and heart-based support. And most of all, I wish to thank my father, who passed during the editing of this book, and my mother for all the invaluable gifts they have given me.

About the Author

Keith Martin-Smith is an award-winning author of numerous fiction and nonfiction books. He is also an ordained Zen priest and a lifelong teacher and practitioner of Chinese martial arts and Qi Gong. He lives in Boulder, Colorado. More at KeithMartinSmith.com.

Index

Pages referencing diagrams are in *italics*.

A
A Heart Blown Open (Martin-Smith), 81, 111
Abraham, 140
abusive relationships, 103, 107–108
acceptance, 22
adrenaline, 90, 145
Adyashanti, 47, 136
allowing, 64
amygdala, 73–74, 77, 89, 90, 145
anger, 7, 90–93, 95
atheism, 6, 27
attachment, 37, 51–53, 61, 87
attunement, 112n29
autonomic nervous system, 72, 74
aversion, 37, 89
awakening
   according to Junpo Denis Kelly Roshi, 64–65, 65n21, 110–111
   as being liberated in world, 46
   and ego, 1, 2
   includes whole you, 151
   as judged by depth of compassion, 22
   no going back from, 44–45
   and problem of ego, 47
   triggers key to, 68
   what it cannot do, 141
   from wheel of life, 155

awareness/enlightenment
   as being awake within, 12
   brings realization of goodness, 148
   and clarity, 11
   defined, 37–40
   disruptive, 132
   includes all reality, 104
   as intimacy with all things, 25
   knowing if enlightened, 139–140
   not bound by time, space or logic, 39
   as only truth, 145–146
   personal experiences of, 28, 30–32
   present before consciousness responds, 115–116
   and spirituality, 13
   steps to choosing, 133–139
   and suffering, 10
   as ultimate subjectivity, 38
ayahuasca, 36, 54

B
Bassui, 147
belief/beliefs, 9, 18–19
biological conditioning, 60, 77–78
Body Keeps the Score: Brain, Mind, and Body in the Healing of Trauma, The (van der Kolk), 71
BRCA1 gene, 60
BRCA2 gene, 60

Buddha, 45, 57, 146
Buddhism, 7, 7n2, 42, 139–140

C
Catcher in the Rye, The, 53
Catholicism, 29, 80
Caulfield, Holden, 53
Chadud Tulka Rinpoche, 42
Chan, 7
China, 7n2
Chögyam Trungpa Rinpoche, 43–44, 43n11, 135
Christ, 32, 140, 146
Christian, 5, 52, 84
clarity, 92–93
cognitive bias, 56
Communism, 25
compassion, 22, 25–26, 148
conditioning, 57–60, 61, 77–78, 82, 144–145. *see also* biological conditioning; culture/cultural conditioning; hysterical-historical conditioning
consciousness, 34–40, 41n10, 47, 53–54, 96
cortex, 72, 75
cortisol, 90, 145
Crichton, Michael, 42
culture/cultural conditioning, 59, 60–61, 67, 106, 107

D
Dalai Lama, 26
Dark Side of the Moon, The, 35
death, 36, 141
Dharma Triangle, 108–110, 108n27, *109*
DMT, 54
DNA testing, 56
Dogen, 12–13, 151
Donne, John, 15
Doshin M.J. Nelson Roshi, 46, 83
Down syndrome, 60
dream yoga, 38, 93
dualism/duality, 128, 129
Dunning-Kruger effect, 56
dysregulation, 72–73

E
Eckhart, Meister, 63
ego
  defined by its thinking, 49–51
  dualistic by nature, 38
  as enemy, 61–62
  hampers awakening, 47
  needed, 22–23
  as process rather than self, 51, 56–57
  required for awakening, 1, 2
  spiritual experiences transcend ego, 6–7
Eido Shimano Roshi, 69, 88
Emerald, David, 108n27
enlightened views, 98, 99, 100
enlightened vs. opinioned, 87–88
enlightening. *see* awareness/enlightenment; surrendering
enmeshment, 112n29
existential anxiety, 36

F
fascists, 24
fawn response, 76–78
fear, 92, 105
feelings/emotions, 89, 92, 97–100, 116
fight or flight, 75–76, *75*
Floyd, George, 151
freeze response, 75–77
Future of the Body, The (Murphy), 42

G
God, 10–11, 63–64, 125, 127–128, 140

H
Hakiun, 40
Heart of Zen, The (Kelly), 13, 13n4, 68–69, 101
Hitler, 50
Holecek, Andrew, 93–94
homophobia, 23
How to Be an Antiracist (Kendi), 24
Humbert, Humbert, 53
hysterical-historical conditioning, 77–78

I
identity, 15, 16–17, 18, 116
ignorance, 37, 88
implicit bias, 56
In the Realm of Hungry Ghosts: Close Encounters with Addiction (Maté), 71
India, 7n2, 59
Innocence Project, 56
insight, 9
integrated views, 100
intolerable situations, 82–83

J
Japan, 7
jealousy, 7, 97

INDEX

Junpo Denis Kelly Roshi
  on awakening, 64–65, 65n21
  on compassion, 22, 25–26, 148
  on conditioning, 77–78, 84
  confronting his childhood, 57, 81
  death of, 151
  devotion to teacher, 88
  on fear, 94
  on feelings as information, 89
  from *In the Heart of Zen*, 101, 139–140
  lineage, 13
  process vs. the self, 51–53
  story about Chögyam Trungpa, 43–44

K

Kendi, Ibram X., 23–24
ketamine, 54, 152
ketamine-assisted therapy (KAT), 84n26
koans/emotional koans, 114–117

L

Lama Tsering Everest, 42, 57
Lao Tzu, 3
liberals, 24–25
liberation
  angst as liberation, 116, 141
  comes from within world, 46, 64–65, 131
  liberation vs. opinion, 20–21
Life of Pi, The, 53
limbic brain, 72, 75
listening, 138–139
Lolita, 53
love, 123
LSD, 54, 57
lust, 7, 97, 128

M

Maharshi, Ramana, 145
Mao, 50
Martin-Smith, Keith
  alcohol and drugs, 33, 80, 84, 152, 154
  atheism, 27
  on Christ and God, 27
  dark night of the self, 152–154
  experiences of mystical awakening, 28, 30–32
  past relationships, 42, 46, 83–84, 92, 152–153
  recollections of childhood, 79–81, 112, 152–154
  on seeing carving of Christ, 32
meditation
  allows one to uncover choice, 95
  as attempt to kill ego, 7
  controlling reactions using, 97
  goal of, 10
  as letting go of need to valuate, 137–138
  as path to enlightenment, 132
  problem with, 70
  slows mind, 82
Mondo Zen, 115

N

Nanquan Puyan, 7
Nazis, 24
neocortex, 90
New York, 127
nonduality, 127–128, 140
Not Knowing, 130, 134–135, 139

O

opinioned vs. enlightened, 87–88
ordinary mind is the way, 7, 25, 48

P

paradox, 3, 6
parasympathetic activation, 74, 75, 75, 77
Patel, Pi, 53
Peter Pan, 76
Philadelphia Shambhala Center, 42
Pink Floyd, 29, 35
Pol Pot, 50
Power of Attachment: How to Create Deep and Lasting Intimate Relationships, The (Levine), 71
process, 51, 53, 55–56, 104, 145
psychotherapy/therapy, 2, 70, 82

R

racial justice theories, 59
racism, 23–24
Ray, Reggie, 135
reality, 50, 144–146
Recovery from Complex PTSD (Barlow), 71
religion, 6, 9, 29, 36, 52
resentment, 92, 144
resistance, 10, 129
Restorative Justice movement, 110
Rinzai Zen, 1, 13

S

scientific reductionism, 6
self, 51, 53, 54–56, 104, 145
Sex, Ecology, Spirituality (Wilber), 41

shadows, psychological, 23, 35, 104, 105
shame, 6, 7, 97
Solzhenitsyn, Aleksandr Isayevich, 25
Song of Zazen, The, 40
Soviet Union, 25
spiritual
  bypassing, 7–8, 68
  identity, 14, 20
  insight, 9, 21, 38, 70, 131–132
  path, 20, 44–45, 61, 147
  practice, 5–6, 7, 14
  self, 146–147
  unfolding, 41
spiritual experiences, 7, 8, 28, 30–32, 131–132. *see also state* experiences
spirituality, 2, 6, 8–9, 13, 88
Stalin, 50
state experiences, 27, 36
Stumbling on Happiness (Gilbert), 54
suffering
  approach to, 140
  cause of, 57, 144
  liberation from, 4, 18
  resistance leads to, 10
  in world, 129
surrendering, 88, 140, 149
survivor, 108
Suzuki Roshi, 128
sympathetic activation, 74–75, *75*, 77

T

Tao Te Ching (Mitchell, trans.), 3
the diamond is in your pocket, 63
thoughts, 16–17
Tibet, 7
Tolle, Eckhart, 46, 47
transformation versus eradication, 24–25
trans-rights movement, 60
trauma, 71–73, 77–78, 82
Travels (Crichton), 42
triggering, *96*, 115, 141
triune brain, 72
Trump, Donald, 151
Trumpism, 24
truth, 47, 50, 145–146

U

unenlightened views, 97, 99, 100
unreliable narrator, 53

V

Vajrayana tradition, 42

van der Kolk, Bessel, 77–79, 81
victimization, 105–110, 108n27, *109*, 113

W

Waking the Tiger: Healing Trauma (Levine), 73
Wilber, Ken, 41–42, 41n10, 48

Z

Zen
  allows all to be, 63
  assessment by Junpo Denis Kelly Roshi, 67
  bypassing triggers, 95
  distinction between relative and absolute, 15
  and enlightenment, 11
  enlightenment as gateless gate, 11, 131
  foundational practices, 64
  Mondo Zen, 115
  perspective on teachers, 88
  Rinzai Zen, 1, 13
  three poisons of the mind, 37

www.ingramcontent.com/pod-product-compliance
Lightning Source LLC
Chambersburg PA
CBHW070151100426
42743CB00013B/2882